May All Your Dreams

Not

Come True

Bob Wilson

All Scripture quotations, unless indicated, are taken from the NEW AMERICAN STANDARD BIBLE. "Scripture quotations taken from the New American Standard Bible®, Copyright © 1960, 1962, 1963, 1968, 1971, 1972, 1973, 1975, 1977, 1995 by The Lockman Foundation. Used by permission." (www.Lockman.org)

The following is a list of other Bible versions used:
Holy Bible from the Ancient Eastern Text. George M. Lamsa's Translations from the Aramaic of the Peshitta. Harper & Row Publishers.

Scripture taken from the HOLY BIBLE, NEW INTERNATIONAL VERSION®. NIV®. Copyright©1973, 1978, 1984 by International Bible Society. Used by permission of Zondervan. All rights reserved.

King James Version. Used by permission of Hendrickson Publishing, Peabody, MA: 2003. All rights reserved.

The Holy Bible, New King James Version. Copyright 1982 by Thomas Nelson, Inc.

All word definitions cited from *The American Heritage College Dictionary*. Houghton Mifflin Company, Boston MA: 1993. All rights reserved.

Printed in the United States of America

Published by WingSpan Press, Livermore, CA
www.wingspanpress.com

The WingSpan name, logo and colophon are the trademarks of WingSpan Publishing.

EAN 978-1-59594-069-8

ISBN 1-59594-069-3

Library of Congress Control Number: 2006905506

To my dearest Ros(ey) who keeps my head shaking, side splitting, and heart singing. To Sonja and Celise, the two angels that I get to share with the world. To my biological and spiritual family scattered throughout the country and to all the people that touched my life around the world.

Contents

Acknowledgments

Writing this book was indeed a daunting task. There were so many thoughts and life experiences to narrow down and try to express. The thought of thanking only a handful of the thousands of people that have influenced my life is almost as daunting as writing this book. I have been profoundly influenced by encounters as intimate as learning about life from my big brother Steve, to an encounter with a complete stranger who helped me find my way in the middle of Africa. Nonetheless, I do want to thank the people who had a specific impact on the completion of this particular journey.

First, to my beloved RoseMary, who is not only one of my biggest encouragers, but was there to give me the constructive critique that I desperately needed.

Next, I am so grateful to have been led to Stephanie Demorest. Having a book edited is a difficult and personal process. Stephanie, thanks for using your red pen with a gentle hand. You were a caring editor and instructor.

My heartfelt gratitude is also felt for the best group of unpaid proofreaders in my life. I would have been truly bewildered without the insight of Lenore Schindler. Then there is Molly Moore who asked me on more than one occasion, "What in the world are you trying to say?" She only laughed out loud twice at my silly semantics. Molly thanks for your self control. To Dana Perkins who only had to read a few chapters before reminding me to make the story personal. I also want to give thanks, and apologize, to Douglas Jacoby. Doug, I thank you for taking the time to read an excerpt and for giving me your astute commentary. I apologize as well for the initial ramblings which were so poorly written (your positive feedback was a true testimony of your kindness).

To my sister Marsha, who is the only proofreader who offered to pay me for her work (if I would bring Celise and Sonja with me). You were a blessing to the compilation of this book and you are a blessing to my life! Please tell your patient husband (my favorite brother-in-law) that all proceeds from this book will be deposited directly into his account.

Next there is my dear friend, David Finnell, who told me in a loving way that he didn't have time to read my book, but if it was a reflection of my heart then it would be very special. David, thank you for telling me what I want to hear, and even what I need to hear at times.

To Lee Boger for leading me to a publishing source and for passing on some of the time that someone shared with him as he compiled his book. And to David Bercot whose books, tapes, and personal pilgrimage have greatly moved my heart and life.

And last but not least, to my mom and dad. Your constant support, encouragement and love for me are beyond what I am capable of expressing. Thank you for bringing me into this crazy world and for trying to protect me from it.

Introductory Greeting

If the book we are reading does not wake us, as with a fist hammering on our skulls, then why do we read it? Good God, we also would be happy if we had no books and such books that make us happy we could, if need be, write ourselves. What we must have are those books that come on us like ill fortune, like the death of one we love better than ourselves, like suicide. A book must be an axe to break the sea frozen inside us.

Franz Kafka

Since I stake my whole life on *The Truth*, let me begin with the truth of why I began to write what in time transformed into this book. I began writing as personal therapy. As my spiritual needs began to be met, the idea of answering other people's inner yearnings stirred a passion in me like I haven't felt in some time.

In 1994, soon after a two-year trip around the world, someone asked me to write a book. Writing a book at that time would have been motivated by one of two reasons: (1) to stroke my over-inflated ego or (2) to make money. Not that I had a true artist's mentality at that time, but it was easy to conclude that neither of these motivations was right. Today my heart and motivations are in a better place: I simply desire to somehow impact people in an intimate way.

I am not a scholar, psychologist, doctor, theologian, self-help guru, and most definitely not a writer. I am a very common man raised and educated in the Midwest. I spent years traveling on business trips staying in four and five-star hotels and spent about the same number of years living in a van, following, among other things, the Grateful Dead. I was also blessed to travel the world and witness various cultures and peoples' lifestyles. I spent years as an agnostic trying to convince myself to be an atheist and lived a year as a full-time Christian minister. Before and along *the way*, I have been inspired by hundreds of books while being impacted by thousands of other writings as well. Of utmost importance, I have examined most religions known to western societies and have come to believe in and, for the last eleven years, to follow *the one* who claims He is God. All of these experiences have enriched my life and learning beyond what any formal education ever could.

Through all of this and many other life experiences that I will share in this book, I have witnessed countless people searching for happiness, love, and ultimately contentment in this crazy world that we have all contributed to shaping. The common denominator for most people could be termed the *ways of the world*. This prevalent choice is not yielding positive eternal results for anyone. American society has created more pills, self-help books, tapes, seminars, talk shows and other forms of psychological babble to make people happy, and yet people seem less and less content. The more alternatives created to help people *feel* young, beautiful, happy, and even pseudo-spiritual, the more people seem to crave and the less content they appear to become.

I am a simple man who has believed for years that the world we have contributed to shaping is way too ugly. More importantly, I have come to terms with the fact that my own heart is much too ugly. I am allowing my heart to be changed by examining it more, and I am changing my world by being consumed by it less. This book doesn't have all the answers (that book has already been written). It is simply the account of one man's journey and immersion around, through, and in the world. It is the story of that same man's desperate attempt to divest his heart from this world and live for something greater than himself.

True writing at its essence is storytelling. You are holding the thoughts, stories, convictions and truths that have flowed from my life experiences, spiritual awakenings and from countless mistakes made. These have formed a story of a yearning heart. I want to share some of these life experiences and a small portion of the mistakes made along the pilgrimage. The limited wisdom from my story could not begin to cut through all of the psychological or self-help promises we have been subjected to throughout our lives, but I hope it is a positive beginning. We are all responsible for our endings, but I believe we can help one another brave new beginnings. My heart's desire is that something in my story reshapes your story and changes it *deeply and eternally*.

Along with my story, I am excited to share many quotes and sound principles. I believe we need to be reminded to follow the tried and true before we try to invent new paths unto the narrow road of contentment. In this spirit I will share some of the thoughts and convictions that have spurred many toward a deeper life. When author Thomas W. Higgins was asked if a certain writing of his was original, he humbly conceded.

> *"Originality is simply a pair of fresh eyes."*[1]

Maybe you will recognize some of the thoughts and convictions presented. I hope reading them in whatever light I can provide will turn your recognition into conviction and therefore action. For some reason you were pulled to look at or invest in my small written contribution. If you are truly searching for answers, you may find them in this book or *The Book* it leads you to discover. As you are seeking answers to your questions, you just might find *The Answer.*

1

It's My Fault

There are plenty of recommendations on how to get out of trouble cheaply and fast. Most of them come down to this: Deny your responsibility.

Lyndon Baines Johnson

President LBJ was scratching a surface that has become a huge infected sore in American society. It is easier to deny your responsibility than to deny yourself and accept whatever responsibility a specific circumstance requires you to own.

There is a good chance that while I was typing the above thoughts more disorders were identified and labeled in the United States and other western societies. Once the disorder or better yet a full-fledged disease is created, planning immediately begins for production of another colored pill, along with a large-scale marketing campaign. Even with that said, I still don't believe that pharmaceutical companies are the core problem.

The root of the issue lies dormant in each of us, waiting to proclaim, "This problem is not my fault." Therefore, I shouldn't have to deal with the responsibility. Don't misinterpret the above analysis for a lack of compassion concerning people in our society with real mental

100 % self responsibility

or physical issues; although, at this point, due to the over saturation of diseases, disorders, and prescription drugs into our culture it may be difficult for us to determine who actually has a problem.

Nor will you see me at the anti-big corporation and/or anti-capitalism protest. Many of us old-timers wouldn't even be alive without some of the remedies that have been created in the past fifty to one hundred years by profit driven companies. My two-year-old daughter was recently diagnosed with scarlet fever. Three days later she was in our back yard digging up plants with her mom. Just over a hundred years ago, we could have been digging her grave in the back yard.

If you are still alive and don't like living in a capitalistic society, you are free to move somewhere more socialistic, communistic, or some other form of-istic. Along with your citizenship, be prepared to hand over most of your money and freedoms you have enjoyed here in America. My point is this: stop wasting energy fighting against big sources that are only a small source of the problem, and begin to take responsibility for your *circumstances*.

It is my fault! Say it with me: it is my fault. Be honest: at some level, it feels good and **right to take responsibility**, even if it is simply words at this point. You may be fighting my premise at this time. If so, let me encourage you with some negative talk about the evils of our society. Keep in mind though, that as you are enjoying this brief time of blame shifting and projecting responsibility onto our big bad evil society, we in some way have contributed to the creation of the mess around us.

Let's take a look at our mess. I would warn you about the shocking nature of the following realities, but we are rarely shocked anymore as a society, and even more frighteningly as individuals. We don't need to research the exact statistics to know that we are living in the midst of a moral epidemic, but here are just a few of the problems that made the upward trend list: pornography, sexual immorality, molestation, pre-teen as well as teen sex and pregnancy, adultery, divorce, child abuse, broken homes, violence, murder, personal debt, financial bankruptcy, and an overall moral decay so immodestly displayed on our televisions, movie screens, school grounds, and in *our churches*.

Have I mentioned yet that this was designed to be an encouraging book? Perhaps you do feel better on some level when reading the above facts. Maybe you, like I, for years either subconsciously or at times consciously felt that you weren't as bad as the people making the above trends. I spent years buying into the world's justifications and excuses. Listed below are some of my favorite excuses that I accepted as absolute truth from the airwaves, television, bookshelves, and most alarmingly from our schools and universities. Our modern society as a whole seems to subscribe to these four propagandized principles for escaping personal responsibility. Please feel free to add any excuses you have identified and possibly used.

1. It is not my fault.
2. My actions do not hurt anybody else.
3. I'm entitled.
4. It is someone else's responsibility.

As for the first excuse, my current conviction is that "it" (whatever "it" is being experienced) is in some way my fault. Even if I or someone else could analyze my circumstance and conclude that it is someone or something else's fault, I still can and need to take responsibility. We must *accept accountability* as we are dealing with our problems, even if the source of a particular issue lies elsewhere.

Secondly, the actions I choose to take have an effect on other people. My responses to any given circumstance, regardless of how or why it was created, have either a positive or negative effect on people. My wife, children, friends, neighbors, and society as a whole are affected by my responses and actions. What is scarier, or more exciting, depending on your outlook, is that the impact of our behavior can be contagious. Thomas Jefferson impacted me greatly with this one sentence sermon:

"It is in our lives and not our words that our religion must be read."

Those closest to us are reading and being impacted by the book that we write daily. We must drink deeply of this timeless phenomena and relish the opportunities each of us have today to inspire ourselves and those we need to love.

The third excuse, regarding entitlement, deserves its own upcoming chapter. For now, a few comments provide the general idea. I am not entitled to anything! You are not entitled to anything! We are not entitled to anything! There will be more on entitlement later, after I go out and purchase a bigger soapbox.

Finally, who needs to take responsibility for the good, bad, and ugly that life presents to us? The following definition of the term *responsible* wakes us to the moral ramifications of our responsibilities:

"Liable to be required to give account, as of one's actions. Able to make moral or rational decisions and therefore answerable for one's behavior."

This definition doesn't easily mesh with the attitude that is so prevalent in our society. We have all seen or had the attitude that says why not pin the responsibilities on someone else, or even something else, if we can't find a human scapegoat.

Here are a few of the most popular scapegoats: parents, family, husband, wife, President Bush, republicans, democrats, pharmaceutical companies, trial lawyers, corporate America, America (the big bully of the world), or maybe more personally "Butch" (the big bully on the elementary school playground who picked on you). Choose one and feel better for about five minutes until you realize deep in your gut that it is not the fault of anything or anyone on your list. And even if a small portion of the blame is someone else's to bear, you have the distinct opportunity and responsibility to deal with that circumstance.

Obviously, our society would be stronger morally if we didn't have advertisements broadcasting the ease of filing for bankruptcy, securing divorce, or gaining a big settlement from some popular targeted scapegoat. We may be better off if advertising campaigns of pharmaceutical companies weren't one of the main sources of diagnosing our medical problems.

As far as you and I should be concerned, it is not the responsibility of any company, profession, or individual to save us from the morally bankrupt society in which we live. It is our responsibility! It is my responsibility! Say it with me if you want to begin traveling on the road which can *change the way* you view your present circumstances. It has taken me years to accept the fact that my life is my responsibility. It is not my minister's responsibility to get my family to heaven, although I appreciate and accept his help. It is not Dr. Phil's responsibility to raise my kids or make sure my marriage is vibrant and growing. Again, I will take solid input from anyone, but ultimately the responsibility rests squarely on my weak shoulders.

At this point you have a strong taste of my convictions concerning entitlement and responsibility. I understand that my approach will not solve all of the world's problems. I can't even seem to solve some of my own. Nonetheless, there simply has to be a better way to be truly happy and content than what the world is offering. If you are searching for the perfect plan, you are in the wrong book. If you are looking for a book that agrees with all your pre-conceived thoughts, neither this nor any other writing will fulfill that wish. The fact is that people can't even agree on The Book with the perfect plan. Nevertheless, I am convinced there are answers for anyone who reads this book with an open disposition. If you can't find answers to your questions, feel free to borrow a question that may lead you to The Answer. The title of the next chapter may be a good initial question to borrow and act upon.

Take courage and believe that we have the power today to break ranks with the world's failed solutions. **Accept and embrace** the reality that we are not entitled, but we are responsible. The way in which we respond to our God-given responsibilities can have an incredibly positive impact on those we love and on this world we so desperately want to change. As Dietrich Bonhoffer was wrestling with the decision to stand up against the Nazi death camps of WWII, he wrote the following call to action.

"Action springs not from thought, but from a readiness for responsibility."[2]

2

How is the World Working for You?

Let me begin with an attempt to succinctly define the terms world, worldly-minded, and world-weary. First, the **world**, for our purposes, refers to things pertaining to secular life and its concerns. **Worldly-minded** means absorbed in the affairs of the world. Finally, **world-weary** means tired of the world.

How is the world working for you? Before answering that or trying to determine your specific absorption into the world, let me apologize for the nature of the question. I hate just about any question that begins with how is the _____ working for you. Usually someone asks the dreaded question in the first place because whatever is being asked is not working well for me at that particular junction of life. When I actually have the *courage to examine the question*, I am oftentimes taken to a place that my heart doesn't like to go.

My second apology is that I have asked you a trick question. I do not believe the world is supposed to work for us. I know for sure that the world is not required to work for us. Did I already write that you and I are not entitled to anything from the world? My daughter Celise came home from kindergarten one day and told me she had experienced short-term memory loss at school and it was very scary (she couldn't think of an answer to a question). I think I may suffer from short-term memory loss and forget that I have already written that we are not entitled!

Let us return to the issue of the world not working for us. Actually, I don't really know what the world is supposed to do or not do for us. Here is what I do know: true happiness, which is **contentment**, is not attained when our hearts are immersed in the world. Contentment is not possible unless we view our short lifetime in this world as a time of training and transition, i.e. a time for us to become less, and for something greater to become more in our lives. I borrowed that thought from the Apostle John. Behold John 3:30!

> *"He must increase, but I must decrease."*

How do we really respond to becoming less? Are we content following this portion of the Scriptures? One definition of **content** is "ready to accept or *acquiesce*; willing." I didn't really know what acquiesce meant either, so I looked up its definition: "to consent or comply passively or without protest." I apologize for looking that acrid word up (the word acrid can be found on the same page with acquiesce).

Are we content to become less in the world? Do we live for worldly attainment and recognition, *or* have we wholeheartedly given our lives to Christ, for whatever purpose He deems necessary? I know the right answer, but actually living it is a daily battle for me. **Living the answer is where contentment awaits!**

Let me state for the record that I don't expect anyone to agree with all my thoughts and convictions, although it would be strange if we didn't agree on some points. Can we agree on the basic premise that what the world is offering to people in their quest for true happiness is not working? What does the world promise?

- ✓ Easy…**money**…
- ✓ Personal…**success**…
- ✓ More…**security**…
- ✓ Looking…**younger**…
- ✓ Living…**longer**…

Even if the promise is realized, it will not necessarily make one happy, nor most importantly, content.

How can we not be so tantalized with the world's empty promises? So what can we do to stop or slow down the degradation the world tries to spoon-feed us everyday? We can begin by not watching it, listening to it, and accepting it like a bunch of laboratory mice. Sometimes you have to be perceived as an outcast or even a neanderthal and take a stand for common decency.

I believe there are millions of people in this country alone, including myself, who are fed up with the world's debasement. We are also incensed by the fact that small, politically correct groups have been silencing the voices of common decency and gut-level spiritual sense for far too many years. I encourage fighting political correctness around every lying turn, but brace yourself for the reality that you and I are not going to change this world by fighting with the weapons created by this world (Ephesians 6:10–17).

So we can't change the world, huh? This is coming from a man who is not a fatalist by nature. I believe that all of our actions have some kind of impact on those around us and, to a lesser degree, the society in which we live. Why would I make such a fatalistic statement? Because we cannot change something that does not want to be changed. I also believe that the evil forces of the world are diametrically opposed to most people's sense of common decency. Wow, that sounds depressing.

Actually knowing the state of the world and our inability to change it is not depressing to me, but rather, *liberating*. I believe this because I am convinced we were not created to change the world to be a little better place to live. Each of us was *created to turn people away* from the world, and *toward God*. Yes we need to live in the world, but we were not designed to be products of it. The world was not designed to work for us and we were not designed to work exclusively for this world.

Don't miss my point. We need to help people. It is praiseworthy to help people work toward short-term solutions in the world to make their temporary residency a bit more tolerable. However, this alone cannot be the ultimate purpose in our lives. Our purpose needs to begin with the impermanent solutions to help our worldwide neighbors have their basic needs met, but let's not leave them there bewildered and possibly lost. After we have helped someone with his physical need, let's help him into a *true biblical relationship* with the One who has called us out of the world.

The beginning of the liberation I spoke of in the previous paragraph can be realized the moment we conclude that we don't need the world to work for us. Where does one find the end of the liberation? Since you were nice enough to invest in this book, I am going to share *The Answer* with you soon. I literally searched around the world trying to find the way I was supposed to work for the world and the way it was supposed to work for me. Allow me to save you some time, money, and heartache, because the liberation to your destined spiritual home can be reached from the physical address at which you currently reside.

3

Around the World for Truth

*A man travels the world over in search of what he needs and
returns home to find it.*

George Moore

Moore's personal discovery literally applies to my past pursuit for
answers. I spent years traveling the world searching after some form
of truth. In retrospect, I realize that the search was not for absolute
truth, but rather, for something that would fit into my *preconceived
ideas* and *comfortable lifestyle*. Was I running after truth or running
from the realization of my miserable discontentment, which I had
experienced up to that point in my life? I had attained everything *in
the world* that I thought would make me happy, and yet I couldn't
seem to fill an ever-expanding void in my heart and life.

Maybe the light that would shine some understanding on the void
and somehow fill it could be found on some distant shore? Perhaps
you haven't done anything as adventurous or foolish as traveling
around the world to find what is probably on your bookshelf, but
are you tired of bouncing from one thing to another, seeking after
an elusive hope for contentment? Have you tried different teachings,
philosophies, self-help ideas, relationships, diets, jobs, or addresses?
There are *so many choices* in the world.

Cringe with me as we look at some of the ways I have grasped after the *oxymoron* known as *contentment in the world*. I spent a couple of years reading hundreds of different philosophies from Confucius to our modern-day confusion. I invested a considerable amount of time and money reading the latest self-help concoctions. For a short while, I even followed after a self-proclaimed prophet, trying to live in "the now." All those "now's" are now part of my wasted past. I did learn during this time that I had a big ego. Wow, maybe he truly was a prophet!

I claimed to be an atheist for awhile and then progressed, if you will, to taking the label of agnostic. I realized that one is a sham and the other is a cop-out (it really doesn't matter which is which). I tried for a few days to fill my life with only pleasant, positive things, but realized I had to leave my apartment and get some groceries. I tried hallucinogenic drugs to experience true happiness, but I can't seem to remember any happiness I may have experienced. I thought knowledge was the key for awhile, but I soon realized that being smart is not one of my gifts. I pursued my vision of the American dream and actually attained it, but I quickly came to understand that the dream was actually a disguised nightmare of discontentment.

Finally, I explored various religions in an effort to find something that would fit into *my* comfortable life. At other times, I found myself seeking something *truly radical*. I discovered that the comfortable life is not very radical and the radical life is rarely comfortable. At some point during this decade-long search, I was unwittingly exposed to a man who was more radical than all other men and their religions combined. Something strange about this *radical one* wouldn't allow me to fit any of the other religions into my life of comfort. There are so many choices in the world! Yet there is only *one true option*. There are so many truths. But there is only **one Truth**!

There were only three things missing in my life before I found *The Truth*:

1. Someone bigger than me to love.
2. Something eternally meaningful to do.
3. Anything to hope for that would endure the test of time.

I guess I was doing okay in my search, if one did not consider eternal love, purpose, and hope. I chose so many of the world's options, trying to fulfill the above three, although at the time I wasn't able to identify the eternal pieces that were missing. There are so many choices in the world!

There are so many choices, but there is only one true option for eternal returns on our time, resources, and energies. Years ago I saw a movie called City Slickers. I loved the advice Jack Palance's character gave to Billy Crystal's character. Here is my paraphrased version: "Find the one thing that will make you truly happy and pursue it with passion." Although I like the idea, I have to disagree with the premise that the one thing chosen can be something different or unique for each person. Actually, the One thing is the same, but *He* works uniquely in the life of each individual who has the courage to choose Him.

There are so many choices in the world! What would you choose? What have you *really chosen*? Consider and answer these questions carefully.

I suspect most people would choose love. People literally search hundreds of paths in the world for love—passionate love. We look for love for or from other people, and even more intimately, love for or from one person. Perhaps we also desire to find a job, hobby, or place that we love. I am convinced that what we desire most is to fill a yearning for a loving relationship with someone.

One of the main issues with love and passion is that they are fleeting because there are human feelings involved. Have you ever had a passion for someone, and the same feelings were not reciprocated? That certain someone wasn't there when you really needed him or her emotionally. I could write another book about all the times someone, or even something, promised to fill my void of love. I could write a separate book about all the times someone's lack of love or carelessness caused me to be hurt and to begin to slowly lose my confidence in receiving fulfillment from worldly love.

Unfortunately, others could write twice as many books about all the times I wasn't there at the right time or usually not there at all for the people I professed to love. I am not going to write those books, and I hope no one that I have let down chooses to write any either. We could all spend too much of our short lives replaying the negative records of our lives, or we can accept the truth and realize that what we love and think we want is ever-changing and temporary, but the One who loves us and is capable of fulfilling our deepest needs never changes. This overwhelming, passionate, and consistent love was, is, and will always be exactly what we are *truly searching for*.

"Jesus Christ is the same yesterday and today, yes and forever" (Hebrews 13:8).

I recently met a man at a conference and asked him how he had passion for the business venture we are both pursuing. I must admit that I didn't grow up dreaming of pursuing my current business endeavor. He shrewdly answered, "I get my passion by thinking of the alternative: feeling pressure from a company to sell more, making money for someone else, and not being able to dictate my own schedule." Thinking of what could be the business alternative in his life has helped him to be more passionate about his current pursuit.

A passion for the Truth (if I can be politically incorrect for a moment, let me narrowly define Truth as Jesus Christ) could begin or be rekindled by thinking of the alternative. I am not just talking about the alternative to heaven, but if contemplating hell ignites an initial passion within you, then allow God to light that flame. What I am really talking about is the alternative of a life of being lured from one worldly passion to another worldly passion. The alternative to this attempt to find the one thing that may make us happier for a few hours, days, or the short life we have, is to find the Truth that gives full joy now and for all eternity.

Truth is at hand. In fact, God desires for you to reach out and take His hand. Stop searching in the world for truth. Let *The Truth* provide you with the answers. At this moment, we are so close to *The Answer* regardless of where we are in the world physically, emotionally, or spiritually. There are so many choices in life, but only one true answer. We can *choose* the way of *truth and true life*, or we can choose to live somewhere lost in the world.

4

Lost Somewhere in the World

I can't say I was ever lost in the woods, but I was bewildered once for three days.

Daniel Boone

Do you ever feel lost in the world? Do the world's standards or lack thereof, ever cause you to feel a bit lost or misplaced? At the very least, do you feel bewildered at times? **Bewildered** is defined as being confused or befuddled, with numerous conflicting situations, objects, or statements. I have felt either lost or bewildered for as long as I can remember.

During some of the very low or high peaks of my life, a nagging question would form in my thoughts, heart, or what a few times felt like the core of my soul. *Is this all there is to life here on earth?* This question first formed in my mind in my late high school years. I was at a loss for the answer then and for nearly fifteen years after that.

If I had had a hard life up until that point, maybe the question would have fit my circumstances better. Growing up in Indiana where I experienced the benefits of two parents who loved me deeply, a great brother and sister, plenty of friends, activities, and a faithful beagle hound at my side, I could have been considered for a Norman

Rockwell painting. Maybe you grew up knowing about, or have heard of, Midwest hospitality. My upbringing was like a storybook, with maybe a few pages of dysfunction thrown in. But I was too young and too busy to notice. Essentially, I had all I needed when I needed it.

In my junior high and high school years I was popular because I was active in sports, and I also related well to those who didn't play. I had not a care in the world other than to enjoy life. There was no major life-changing event that occurred in the first eighteen years of my existence. What could have prompted the lingering question in the back of my mind, is this all there is to life? Why, among all the questions in life, did this particular one seem to *require an answer*?

In college I became more free to explore life, and I took full advantage of the newfound freedom. As the old saying goes, "I never let school get in the way of my education." From a worldly perspective, I was living a young man's dream: playing college baseball, partying with no curfew, entertaining beautiful women. I was learning a world previously unknown to me, through new friends from places I had never been. I even learned some cool things in the classroom. The vague quiet question that formed in the back of my brain in high school was making its way toward my heart by the end of my college experience. I also began to have a deeper longing for the answer. I wonder now if some of my college friends were asking or wondering if this is all there is to life...**I wonder if you have ever asked that question.**

After college I moved to San Francisco and within a year made my way to sunny Southern California. I was able to leave behind most everything in the Midwest except for that penetrating question. It had not gotten loud enough at this point for me to stop looking for answers in the same empty places. I hadn't learned the world's definition of insanity yet: "doing the same thing over and over, expecting a different result." Maybe I didn't really want a different result badly enough by this time. I can only surmise that the emptiness that prompted my discontented state wasn't yet large enough.

Just after my twenty-fifth birthday I stumbled into an employment position where I was a sales manager covering twelve Western States and Western Canada. I had the opportunity to frequently travel to Hawaii and to Alaska as well as throughout the above region. I was living on an expense account and was staying and eating in places with more stars than I had ever experienced. On the weekends I had money in the bank and was enjoying many of the beautiful sites of California. How could anyone be unhappy or discontent living such an exciting life?

At this point the question had pervaded my heart completely. I remember one time saying to myself, "God, I hope there is more to this life than all the things with which I am trying to fill it." This verbalization was strange for two reasons: (1) I didn't believe in God at the time, and (2) I wasn't in the habit of talking to myself.

Just before my thirtieth birthday, I set out not only to answer the question, but also to put an end to my overall feeling of being lost in the world. Many may say that I came up with a good, if not perfect, plan. I decided to travel the world and experience other ways of living to see if I had missed, or didn't have access to, the answer. I sold all my possessions except a backpack of necessities and began traveling in an easterly direction. This particular adventure lasted nearly three years and crossed over fifty countries and almost fifty states. I feel grateful and blessed for the lifetime of memories given to me during my travels.

One of the most memorable experiences happened on an exotic island in Indonesia. If I had to picture the ultimate fantasy at that stage of life, it would have included relaxing on a tropical island and observing some of the world's most beautiful creations. How could anyone be lost in the middle of his fantasy? One evening on my "Fantasy Island" in Indonesia, I found myself in an empty youth hostel, crying for only the third or fourth time in my adult life, desperately hoping that this was not all there was to life. I remember thinking and writing in a journal that if this is all there is to life, then shame on the creator.

Maybe the creator finally answered my whimpering, or perhaps I finally began to listen. In this deserted hostel, in the middle of *my nowhere*, a light suddenly came on from the back cleaning closet. An older Indonesian man walked slowly from the light toward *the darkness* where I was sitting. He stopped momentarily, peered through my eyes, and inquired, "Have you ever studied the Bible?" In retrospect, I realize that he didn't seem to be there for an answer. He smiled deeply and firmly placed a well worn New Testament into my damp hands. This is all he ever said to me. Even in my critical condition, I sensed this was more than mere coincidence. Unfortunately, I was so lost and hardhearted at the time that I failed to take his direction. I left the copy of *my answer* at the youth hostel.

Being lost is such a horrible feeling. I still get lost directionally. Usually I won't stop for directions, or when I do stop, I don't really listen. Being lost spiritually is so much more horrible. I traveled the world and never stopped long enough or listened intently enough to find the answer. Nearly two years after a mysterious man had asked me if I had ever studied the Bible, I finally stopped and cried not in self-pity, but for help. God sent a man named Ed Sams, who was offering the perfect directions. I accepted and listened to God's Word intently. I was baptized and saved on July 29, 1994. I haven't been lost eternally since that glorious day!

There is The Way of being found in the world. No, I am not going to ask you to bow and accept Jesus into your heart. I will never ask anyone to be saved in this manner because it is *not the biblical way to salvation!* Jesus expects to be accepted. He demands to be followed and obeyed.

Once we accept and surrender to the demands of Jesus we never have to be lost again. We may have to *admit that we are lost*, which can be extremely difficult for us humans. Once we admit, accept, and *act on our lostness*, then we never have to be lost again. When we choose His way (*The Way*), at last we find *our way*.

The good news is that we don't have to be lost. The not-so-good news is that I haven't fully figured out an escape from the entanglements of the world. I spend way too much time entangled in the world's ways. I have realized that a complete escape from the world is not yet possible, but I can decide to reduce the amount of bewilderment I choose to participate in and accept as necessary.

Are any of these thoughts about being found, or at least less entangled, *speaking to you?* Perhaps you are lost in what I am writing or bewildered by why I am writing. Let me pose a question that may not clarify my point in this chapter, but it may help clarify the point of life. *Are you content?* If you are like I was for many years, you are satisfied with answering *sometimes*. The question requires a *yes or no* answer.

If we aren't content with who, where, and why we are, then we are either lost or have allowed ourselves to be too caught up in the insane playground of the world. The answer to discontentment and being spiritually lost is nearby. Vincent Van Gogh once tried to encourage his brother Theo with this worthy word picture. "If one feels the need of something grand, something infinite, something that makes one feel aware of God, one need not go far to find it."[1]

I believe Theo was encouraged because everyone loves good news. I love it so much I decided to follow *the good news* for the rest of my life. The great thing about following it is that you always have victory around, which comes in handy during the daily battles with and in the world. The world we inhabit can be a scary, downright insane place in which to live. This dark fact would be alarming if not for the following illumination.

The world isn't as frightening after
you have been saved from its insanity.

As Socrates once boldly exclaimed, "The unexamined life is not worth living."

Examine your life! Are you bewildered by or in the world? Are you frightened at all about the end of your life? Obviously, I do not know where you are on life's pendulum of lostness or bewilderment. I hope to inspire each and every reader to find the answers to these questions. The initial goal is that we would all examine our lives *more openly and honestly.*

Will we have the courage to really examine questions such as the following: am I saved in accordance with the Scriptures? Am I devoted to the treasures in the world more than I am devoted to God? Maybe you honestly do not know how you feel about the world or where you stand with God. I want to be here to help guide you in some small way to *the answer.*

Many newer cars have GPS (Global Positioning Satellite) systems to help people find the way to their destinations. God has His own GPS system for people to find His final destination.

GPS: God's plan of salvation.

Keep in mind that the road to God's final destination is very narrow, so we will really have to pay close attention to His directions. Also understand when I use the term "system" it does not refer to a legalistic plan you adhere to like a set of work-related rules and regulations. At the foundation of God's plan is a *living, love relationship* with His Son, Jesus. Without this foundation, we will not be able to *sustain* the desire to be led down His narrow road. We can't simply check off the directions of the GPS system and then get back to our important business in the world.

The following description of God's plan of salvation must become our *business in the world.* This GPS system will last the lifetime of our bodies and souls. Many people and religious institutions have gone against the owner's manual and changed or upgraded (downgraded) God's plan of salvation.

1) *Believe:* Believe that the Bible is God's inspired Word and that He is capable of doing all it says. More specifically, believe that Jesus is *exactly* who he claims to be. He was with God in the beginning. He became man by being born of a virgin. He lived a perfect life, suffered, and was crucified *for and because of* our sins. He rose on the third day and some forty days later rose to be with His Father again in heaven. Oh yes, He is coming back to judge each person's acceptance of and obedience to His Word.

In John 12:48 Jesus says, "He who rejects Me, and does not receive My sayings, has one who judges him; the word I spoke is what will judge him at the last day."

2) *Repent:* This is not just saying I am sorry but includes a 180-degree turn. Stop doing all the things God's Word says to stop, and equally important, try with all your heart to do all the things His Word says to do.

In 2 Corinthians 7:10, 11 the Apostle Paul says, "Godly sorrow brings repentance that leads to salvation and leaves no regret, but worldly sorrow brings death. See what this godly sorrow has produced in you: what earnestness, what eagerness to clear yourselves, what indignation, what alarm, what longing, what concern, what readiness to see justice done. At every point you have proved yourselves to be innocent in this matter" (NIV).

3) *Be Baptized:* The Greek word for baptize means to immerse or dip (in water). Baptism is for the forgiveness of all our sins that we have committed up to the point of being baptized. Baptism also allows us to receive the gift of His Holy Spirit. Cf. Acts 2:36–38! I will say more on baptism later, but I encourage you to read Romans 6:1–4, Ephesians 4:4–6, Mark 16:16, Colossians 2:8–13, John 3:3–6, Acts 22:15, 16 and 1 Peter 3:18–22. *According to the Bible* one does not receive His forgiveness or receive the Holy Spirit when he or she prays or accepts Jesus into his or her heart.

4) *Confess and allow Jesus to be Lord of our lives:* Believing, repenting and being baptized can take hours, days, weeks or longer for a person to understand and obey. The confession part is a lifelong work of surrender. Unfortunately, a majority of individuals and churches in America have scaled back salvation to include only belief in Jesus and *verbalizing* Him as Lord. Confessing Jesus as Lord has been wrapped up *conveniently in a false teaching.* Confessing Jesus as Lord with our mouths at baptism, and with our lives every day, is allowing Him to truly be Lord of our lives! Jesus is Lord of everything: time, money, comforts and dreams. He should be Lord of what we do, how we work, and why we live.

Please read and respond to Luke 14:25–33!

You and I can be lost in the world, but *we cannot be lost in* God's kingdom. We are bewildered sometimes and striving to be closer to Christ daily, yes, but being lost and being part of His kingdom is an oxymoron of eternal proportions.

Where are you? Are you trying to fill a void in your life that can only be filled by God? Have you *simply* "prayed Jesus into your heart?" Did this emotional confession lead to *biblical repentance and baptism*? If so, are you battling daily to allow Jesus to be Lord of your life? This battle is intensely personal because it is waged each day against our *greatest enemy, ourselves.*

The battle of who is truly Lord of our heart and life should lead us to the commandments that call us to be separate from the world. As one studies why and how the apostles and the people of the early church lived and died so radically, something shines forth about these devoted disciples. In heart, spirit, and life they *chose* to separate themselves from the world. In response to questioning from those of the world, a second-century elder of Christ's church expressed the following battle cry on behalf of all true warriors of *the way:*

> "All zeal in the pursuit of glory and honor is dead in us. So we
> have no inducement to take part in your public meetings. Nor

is there anything more entirely foreign to us than the affairs of State (politics). We renounce all your spectacles... Among us, nothing is ever said, seen, or heard that has anything in common with the madness of the circus, the immodesty of the theater, the atrocities of the arena, or the useless exercise of the wrestling ground. Why do you take offense at us because we differ from you in regard to your pleasure?"[2]

As we struggle with His Lordship (allowing Jesus to be in control of every aspect of our lives), we need to wrestle with the Scriptures, ourselves, and Satan to act upon this separation. This battle should encompass our minds, hearts, and lives. God will give us victory as we surrender to Christ and *strive* to separate ourselves for Him alone. Take courage that there are people who are serious about Lordship and separation. I, for one, am striving with all my heart to please my Lord in these two crucial areas. Out of my love for God, I am examining every area of my heart and life to make sure it is surrendered to Christ and His kingdom. *Striving* to separate my heart and life from Satan and his kingdom.

If you are a professing Christian and don't see the need for Lordship and separation from the world, you may want to go back and examine not only God's GPS system but also Jesus' core teachings, such as the Sermon on the Mount (Matthew 5–7). Remember the one we call "Lord" expects to be Lord. Matthew 7:21 soberly states.

> "Not everyone who says to Me, Lord, Lord,
> will enter the kingdom of heaven; but he who
> does the will of My Father who is in heaven."

If you think all of the above is a bunch of nonsense, I would simply ask you to continue to explore this radical and magnificent one that many call Jesus and that I call Lord. If you are not open-minded enough to explore Jesus further, I would encourage you to be the best person you can be in your own power. Please try not to guide anyone away from the safety of God's GPS system. My hope is to save you a lot of time, money and heartache by convincing you that there is only one road out of the deep, dark void of discontentment that the world offers.

I must also report that many smarter people than you and I believe that the yearning for God is beyond our control.

Blaise Pascal, the French mathematician who developed the modern theory of probability, discovered the definitive solution: "There is a God-shaped vacuum in the heart of each man which cannot be satisfied by any created thing, but only by God, the creator, made known through Jesus Christ."[3]

Augustine aptly prayed these words of peace: "Thou hast made us for thyself, O' Lord, and our hearts are restless until they find their rest in thee."[4]

In Ecclesiastes 3:11, we find that God sets eternity on the hearts of mankind. (Paraphrased from the NIV)

That yearning for more is present in us all. The deep inner desire to fill the massive void created by the world is not a concept that Pascal, Augustine, or thousands of other writers have discovered. I am not sure why God put eternity on the hearts of people, but I do know that this yearning can be an incredible blessing or curse, depending on how one tries to fill this ever-expanding void.

Speaking very personally, it has been both a blessing and curse to me. For thirty-two years I allowed myself to be cursed by being desperately lost in the world. I tried anything and almost everything to fill the God-shaped vacuum. One of the millions of blessings of choosing to be found is that I don't have to helplessly and hopelessly try to fill up the vacuum anymore. The joys of personal salvation are difficult at times for me to express, but the following utterance gives a universal understanding:

Salvation is being saved from disaster, fear, hunger and a meaningless life. It is being saved for hope, love, security and the fulfillment of purpose.

In a sense we have all been found. As these words of C.S Lewis continue to remind us, "If Shakespeare and Hamlet could ever meet it would be Shakespeare's doing." God has already made himself known. His invitation in the form of Jesus was sent, suffered, and sacrificed for our salvation. In the spirit of freedom and fair play, God gives us the *ultimate decision* to be found or to continue to be lost. You and I are not entitled to the ultimate void-filler called salvation, but God is eager to fill us with His gift.

5

Only God is Entitled

Gratitude unlocks the fullness of life. It turns what we have into enough and more. It turns denial into acceptance, chaos to order, confusion to clarity. It can turn a meal into a feast, a house into a home, a stranger into a friend. Gratitude makes sense of our past, brings peace for today, and creates a vision for tomorrow.

Melody Beattie

Gratitude is a building block very near the foundation of contentment. I have found that ingratitude frequently follows closely behind an *attitude of entitlement*. A grateful heart doesn't expect gifts of entitlement. We actually do deserve something, but trust me, we do not really want what we should be entitled to receive. In a journal entry sometime in the year 2004, I wrote the following about the reception Jesus received during his physical visit to earth:

The Lord Jesus Christ was humiliated, spit on, beaten, lied about, lied to and despised. Born on earth in a cave and began his life with his parents fleeing to Egypt, to avoid the baby's death. He ended his life by resolutely walking into Jerusalem to face not only his death, but ours as well. (Luke 13:31–33). Throughout his entire life Jesus humbled himself and even allowed man to humble him. He spoke to the destitute and ate with prostitutes. Jesus is not ashamed to call anyone a brother who simply follows the same path of humility and obedience that he learned to endure. (Isaiah 53:1–7).

Humiliated by his hometown, many of his own race and his own family. Deserted by his disciples during his greatest hour of need. No one on earth truly understood him. Jesus was in heaven with God, being part of God. He set aside this privilege and came to earth for man, became part of man, i.e. human!

Philippians 2:3–8: "Do nothing from selfishness or empty conceit, but with humility of mind let each of you regard one another as more important than himself; do not merely look out for your own personal interests, but also for the interests of others. Have this attitude in yourselves which was also in Christ Jesus, who, although he existed in the form of God, did not regard equality with God a thing to be grasped, but emptied himself, taking the form of a bond-servant, and being made in the likeness of men. And being found in appearance as a man, he humbled himself by becoming obedient to the point of death, even death on a cross."

Baptized by man and rejected by men. Doubted, tested, not trusted, entrapped and abandoned. He had no one on earth to confide in while he knew his eventual doom. Mocked, ridiculed, called insane and accused of being Satan. Tortured, stripped, betrayed, denied and hated by the masses. Thirty three years of hell on earth! The humiliation of being around sinful people that he helped create. Dependent on these same deceitful people to meet his physical needs. Any man would have been tempted to think, why did I come to earth? Why did I create this? The only man in history undeserving of any punishment. An innocent lamb led to the slaughter.

I share this very incomplete depiction of the suffering of Jesus to help us focus on what we really deserve for the millions of sins we have committed and continue to commit. To what should our countless acts of pure unadulterated selfishness and wickedness entitle us? The simple act of reminding ourselves of what we really deserve would *radically change* our lives and the lives of most people around us in incredible ways.

It seems obvious to me that we shouldn't feel entitled to worldly benefits like healthcare, employment, housing; in my view we are not entitled to anything. If we would accept and embrace this view, we would start being much more grateful for all the incredible blessings God provides. Reread my brief, incomplete description of the suffering Jesus experienced. Better yet, write your own description. On a separate sheet of paper write out a list of a hundred or so sinful thoughts and acts you have committed during the past week. By the time we have finished the page describing Jesus it should be covered with tears of *gratitude*; the page describing us can be covered by **His blood!**

The only man in history who could have made a winning argument for deserving special treatment received nothing but pain and torment while he walked the earth. If the one who created and sustains everything didn't receive any earthly entitlements, then how can we expect to feel or be entitled?

For the sake of argument, remove religion from the equation for a moment and reflect on the benefits of being born a human being. Assuming you live in America, ponder for a moment the freedom and material comforts you enjoy. How much did you contribute toward your birth? How much did you pitch in for the first eighteen years of your life? Even at this point, we should clearly see that we don't deserve much. In fact, I would avoid bringing up the subject because we will always lose our justification debate about deserving more. I choose to keep quiet and continue to accept all the gifts I am not entitled to.

In 2004 my net pay out in federal and state income taxes was approximately $3,000. Do you think I used $3,000 worth of protection and services? How much is it worth to have our families and possessions protected. How much peace of mind alone do the police and fire departments provide? What about the various ways the national government protects us. Are we at $3,000 yet? In case you don't place a high value on peace of mind, what about use of the roadways, schools and landfills?

The point is not to promote any particular government or make us feel guilty about the abundance that we all receive. As a follower of Christ who is called to a life of non-violence, I obviously have issues with some of the policies of all governments. Nor do I go around feeling guilty about what my family receives. The point we need to understand is that we are undeserving of all that we receive. This understanding and conviction will guide us into a more grateful existence.

Begin by being grateful for the hundreds of things we get in the world, and then *graduate to an attitude of gratitude* for the millions of gifts we freely receive from God. A.W. Tozer takes this ungodly attitude of entitlement and fair treatment back to the cross, the place where it must be crucified

Christians who understand the true meaning of the cross will never whine about being treated fairly. Whether or not they are given fair treatment will never enter their heads. They know they have been called to follow Christ, and certainly Christ did not receive anything remotely approaching fair treatment from mankind. Right there lies the glory of the cross—that a man suffered unfairly, was abused and maligned and crucified by people unworthy to breathe the same air with him. Yet he did not open his mouth. Though reviled he did not return the hatred, and when he suffered, he did not threaten anyone. The thought of his shouting for fair play simply *cannot be entertained by the reverent heart.* His whole life was dedicated to restoring that which he had not taken away. Had he sat down and calculated how much he owed and then carefully paid no more, the whole moral universe would have collapsed.[1]

Only God is truly entitled to anything and everything. Remind yourself often of my three laws of entitlement:

1. I am not entitled; only God is entitled
2. I don't deserve anything except punishment and death.
3. I should be grateful for anything and everything I get above nothing.

Henry Ward Beecher wrote, "A proud man is seldom a grateful man, for he never thinks he gets as much as he deserves."[2] James, one of the brothers of Jesus, helps lead us to the foundational issue: "God is opposed to the proud, but gives grace to the humble" (James 4:6b).

You and I need to do the spiritual math of Henry and James and act accordingly. To help us figure out the above spiritual math problem, let's go back together and read the last sentence of the quote that began this chapter.

"Gratitude makes sense of our past, brings peace for today and creates a vision for tomorrow."

Does your past make sense to you? Gratitude will help bring us to our senses and will comfort us with a better understanding. Are you presently at peace? Gratitude is a tireless peacemaker. Do you have a vision for tomorrow? Gratitude can make the future more clear. At the very least it will help you live today in peace and someday your future will pass, and it will all make sense.

6

Time Can Be on Your Side

Measure life in loan payments and time runs out. Measure life by infinite values and time stays out of your way.

Henry David Thoreau

So you never seem to have enough time? You are not alone. A question was posed recently at the church my family attends: Why don't we spend more time with God, with people, and doing those things that Christ commands? The overwhelming response was, "I don't have enough time." Actually, there is an element of truth in that *excuse*. We as a people in America have absolutely allowed ourselves to become too busy with things outside of spending time with God, with people, and acting on the commands of Christ. Are we busy for God or *just too busy?*

The larger element of truth is that the way we choose to spend our time is a *decision*. It can be traced back in most instances to priority and love. Have you ever noticed that we somehow find the time to do the things we *really want to do*. I remember a time a few years ago when I was frustrated because I didn't feel like I had enough time to spend with people. Here is the sadly ironic fact. I had the thought as I was watching my favorite television show.

For many reasons I made a decision to get rid of our television, and it is amazing how much more time I now have because of that one choice. Having more time is a positive start, but it still doesn't address the issue of priority and love. Obviously, we can stop doing something that is *wasting* our time like watching television, but we could easily replace this activity with something not related to God, people, or other ways we should be spending the **time we have been entrusted.**

Here is an idea if you are not comfortable with turning the television off, or perhaps you have become too comfortable to turn it off. I could develop another time saving device or system to address our perceived lack of time. How about some more technology that will give us more time for our spiritual, family and (if there is any time left), personal lives? Let's see…the computer, e-mail, fax machine, microwave, automobile, air travel, television, DVD player, complex phone systems and palm pilot have already been created. These have certainly worked well to free up our schedules for us to build deeper spiritual and family lives, haven't they? I am not advocating going back to the days before the technological revolution. I am simply asking us to step back, evaluate, and rearrange priorities as needed.

What are our priorities? Can I cut off some of the "technological noise," or at least turn it down so I can get about the business of loving God and people? When the noise is turned off or down is a great time to act on those convictions that are lying dormant in our hearts and minds. You know, the ones we never seem to have the time upon which to act. We are not going to have victories in the man-made battles for more time unless we *stop adding* more things, gadgets, and, in some instances even, technology to our lives.

Time was not made for things; it was made for people. We need to ask ourselves simple questions like…is this gadget saving or wasting my time? Does this technology create more non-essential things for me to do or less? Are we making the world so efficient that we have ceased to experience life? As Alice Kahn humorously noted, "For a list of ways technology has failed to improve the quality of life please press 3."[1] I am in agreement with Alice: if technology is going to rob us of our personal relationships, it should at least allow us to talk with someone non-automated on the phone. I am called to love all people, but I must confess that I do not love automated people very much.

Would you really like for me to help you invent more time? It has been said that necessity is the mother of invention. What is *necessary today?* What is really necessary for our relatively few tomorrows we may have left? What is necessary for us to do the rest of our todays so we can enjoy the endless days of eternity? William Penn may have said it best, "Time is what we want most, but what we use worst; and for which God will certainly most strictly reckon with us, when time shall be no more."[2]

Don't look down now, but time is running through your fingers. We can either utilize or waste the *precious gift of time!* How and where are you investing your invaluable gift? In the spirit of the quote opening this chapter, I must ask if we are spending our lives striving to stay caught up on our loan payments or if we are using the time God has entrusted to us on matters of infinite value? *Time* was not made for things; it *was created for people!*

By now you realize that I am trying desperately to pattern my life after Jesus Christ, His apostles, and those crazy followers of the first few centuries. One of the best books, outside of the Bible, that I have ever read is *The Kingdom That Turned the World Upside Down* by David Bercot. Mr. Bercot asks his readers to compare the number of hours per week spent on kingdom interests to the number of hours per week spent working for and taking care of material things. He then poses two questions that have haunted me for months. *I pray they haunt you as well.*

"Where does most of your time go? Obviously, some secular work is necessary to provide for the necessities of life. But do we really think we're going to be able to convince Jesus that we are working only for the necessities of life—not to maintain the comfortable American lifestyle?"[3]

I have wrestled with this question for nearly a year, and I have not won the wrestling match yet. I never participated in the sport of wrestling, but I know that you either win by getting more points than the opponent or by pinning him to the mat. I am not sure if we will ever know, with certainty, if we have pinned the opponent, "wasted time." I fully understand that the question doesn't have a black-and-white answer that fits everyone equally. Therefore, we may not be able to determine if we have pinned this opponent, but we should be able to clearly win the match with more points. It should be *obvious* that we devote the majority of our time to God, others, and the things they need. Marcus Aurelius, at some point in his wrestling match with this daunting opponent called "wasted time," wrote these timeless words. "Time is a sort of river of passing events, and strong is its current; no sooner is a thing brought to site than it is swept by and another takes its place, and this too will be swept away."[4]

If we are true followers of Christ, the temptation to live for the American dream or *anything other* than God's dream is always before us. My counsel is to strive to invest in building God's house larger and more beautiful while saying "no" to most investments that build your own house (Haggai 1:3–11). Just say "yes" to investments that give a high rate of return on relationships. Invest the firstfruits of your time in building a deeper, biblical relationship with God through His Son Jesus. As your relationship with Christ deepens, your connections with people will become *richer.*

My wife, RoseMary, is one of the best examples I know with regard to the above in action. Early each morning, she spends time walking, praying, reading and/or singing to God. I have been blessed to watch her for many years strive for intimacy in her relationship with Christ. She *guards her special times* with passion.

Most people choose to spend their time mastering the latest technology and staying on top of all the worldly gossip. Rosey would rather take the time to teach our two daughters to fall in love with God through nature. She rarely seems to get all the stuff done in her planner, but she usually finds that rare commodity called time to invest in people. Not to be redundant, but my experience is that we seem to always find time to do the things that we *make a priority* in our life.

RoseMary and I are constantly battling with the task of how to use our time to build deeper relationships and ultimately God's kingdom. While most people in America try to build the right financial portfolio, I believe it is so much wiser for people to develop the right *time portfolio*. Here is a suggestion for our time distribution: God 100%; family (spiritual and biological) 30%; useful activities 15%; and personal wants 5%. I know that those numbers total 150%, but if we allow God to guide every aspect of our lives, He will work out the math.

Once you have prayed, sought advice, and talked with your family about the time portfolio, let me suggest an exercise that may help get you kick started. Try cutting out half, i.e. half of your thoughts, half of your planner, and if you are really adventurous, half of your possessions. I believe if you apply the "half exercise," your life could be twice as full, not half as full. Perhaps this seems overwhelming; how about eliminating a quarter, a tenth, or even one useless thought, one non-essential activity, and just one major time-consuming possession. It could be the first of many steps to figuring out what is really important. It could be the beginning of seeing *time as an ally* and not the enemy.

Whatever plan you embark on to restructure your life should lead to more time to focus on relationships. My best friend has inspired the ultimate book on how to spend time building relationships. I would like to introduce him to you. One warning, He believes he is perfect, and if you want to be His friend you have to do exactly what He tells you to do. John 15:14 commands the following condition of friendship: "You are my friends if you do what I command."

7

Jesus is Perfect and I Don't Love Him Enough

This Jesus of Nazareth, without money and weapons conquered more millions than Alexander, Caesar, Mohammed and Napoleon; without science and learning, He shed more light on things human and divine than all philosophers and scholars combined; without the eloquence of schools, He spoke such words of life as were never spoken before or since, and produced effects which lie beyond the reach of orator or poet; without writing a single line, He set more pens in motion, and furnished more themes for sermons, discussions, books, works of art and songs of praise than the whole army of great men of ancient and modern times.

Josh McDowell

If you are not a "professing Christian" or a person who has not previously been open to Christ or His teachings, I admire that you are still reading this book. In my short life I have progressed from claiming to be an atheist to an agnostic to a believer of Christ to an actual follower of His. We have all been affected in some way by the constant subtle and blatant teachings of secularism by institutions of the world. These teachings, along with many others, in our public school systems alone have done some form of lifelong damage to most of us. I simply ask that you continue reading and open your mind for at least a few more pages. Delight and stand amazed at the ultimate radical one called Jesus.

A man once asked me how I could say that Jesus was the most radical person who ever walked the earth. I told him that to be considered for this honor, the person had to have created the world, have the power to sustain it, and have the authority to come back and judge mankind at the end of time. My *radical one* wins by default. Even without all that little stuff like creation or rising from the dead or having the power and authority to raise us from the grave, I still believe He is the most radical of all mankind.

To us who have *surrendered back* the life Jesus gave us, He is so much more than just some radical God/man. He is my big brother who takes care of all the bullies, on the playground of the world, who mess with me. For some wonderful reason, the One who created the universes unknown desired to make Himself known to me. Oh yes, and He is perfect.

Hey, I understand we all get a bit uncomfortable with people who think they are perfect. We may even ask, "Who do they think they are? God's gift to the world?" So when we encounter Jesus for the first time, or anytime for that matter, it is quite overwhelming. He is perfect, and if that isn't enough for one person, He actually is God's gift to the world. Would you like to know how I am certain that He is perfect? No one has ever found anything imperfect about Him, and it is not for a lack of trying. The Roman authorities, the Jewish leaders, and many other people of His day were *unable to find one imperfection.* They couldn't even find His body!

Jesus is love, truth, compassion, hope, life, and the only road to eternal bliss, and I can't seem to love Him enough. What *in the world* am I doing? Christ is the answer! Since He is the answer to every eternal question, He gets to ask the questions. Do you *really* love me? Do you love me *above all* things and all people? When are you planning on surrendering your *entire* life to me? And whatever other questions *the answer* wants to ask.

Jesus is the only "pill" you will probably ever need, but it is a challenging one to swallow everyday. He is not to be fit into our planners; He is the planner! Jesus can't be just a part of our lives. He either encompasses all of my life, or He is not truly a part of it. We cannot have a *casual relationship* with the King of the universe!

What is the point of this chapter? The point is the same as that of this life: JESUS! Every founder of every religion and philosophy, besides Christianity, was unable to pull off one small feat: RESURRECTION FROM THE DEAD! How are you and I supposed to respond to *the one* who rose? We must respond however He tells us to, whether we like it or not. Years ago, I asked my brother, who is in the Air Force, if he struggled to follow the commands of a President who was unpopular with the military. He replied, "My responsibility is not to question the Commander in Chief. He gives the order, and I follow it." This incredible commitment to a flawed man convicts me deeply. What about my devotion to the perfect Commander in Chief of the universe?

Why is it so difficult to follow this Prince of Perfection? I can only speak specifically for myself and give an educated guess regarding why most people don't surrender and devote their lives completely to Jesus. First and foremost, I believe we struggle simply because it is hard! Truly following Jesus is the highest and hardest call anyone will ever be asked to answer. To not just believe or profess, but to truly surrender and follow is the most radical calling on earth. It is relatively *easy to believe in the radical* and profess the radical, but it is a daily war to actually live radically. Giving up everything means giving up everything.

Secondly, most people are confused about God's kingdom. I would surmise that most professing Christians think that one believes in Jesus now and then gets to be in His kingdom when he or she dies. Unlike Jesus, His apostles and the people in the early church, the overwhelming majority of people today don't grasp that there are two kingdoms on earth and we must choose to live for one or the other. People spend most of their life on earth seeking happiness, recognition, worldly security, attainment of a lifestyle, and so many other things in the world that appear worthwhile. People who choose to live for the kingdom of this world choose these goals. They are not the things in which Jesus wants his disciples to seek or find their comfort.

This *doctrine of the two kingdoms* that Jesus and the early followers not only understood, but lived, is a relatively new concept to me. Therefore, I may not be the best person to come to for guidance. In a spiritual nutshell, the universal belief through the early part of the fourth century was that there are two kingdoms battling side by side here on earth: the kingdom of God and the kingdom of the world. A person could only give his or her allegiance to one or the other. I am convinced that this understanding of the early disciples is why they were different from me and anyone I know in the twenty-first century.

The only practical help I can offer is to advise that you start digging through the New Testament with a fresh perspective. Try to forget as much as you can of what you have previously learned. Read it and take it as personally and literally as the Spirit allows. Begin with the *Sermon on the Mount (Gospel of Matthew 5–7; Gospel of Luke 6) and read it again and again and again.* If there was a written constitution of the earliest Christians "this" would be the document.

No, the Sermon on the Mount is not impossible to follow, but it will seem like it. A word of warning, if you choose to truly follow these teachings of Jesus you will be instantly separating yourself from about ninety-nine percent of the world and, in my estimation, about ninety-five percent of "professing Christians." Help is available, and you are going to need guidance. Beyond the above input, I would once again strongly encourage you to read *The Kingdom That Turned the World Upside Down* by David Bercot.

We have examined enough of the practicals. Let us get back to the King Immortal. Do you feel like you have a clearer picture of the Lord Jesus Christ yet? Is He wonderful enough for you and me to be different than the masses? Is the picture clear enough in your heart to fight for the King and His Kingdom? I hope the following heartfelt, yet feeble, attempt to further describe my King will become fighting words for you.

Jesus is the King of Kings and the Lord of Lords. He is sovereign. No means of measure can define His limitless love. No barrier can hinder Him from throwing out His blessings. He is enduringly strong, eternally sincere, immortally gracious, imperially powerful and impartially merciful. This King has made Himself known.

I wonder how well we *really know Him*.

Jesus is the greatest phenomenon who ever crossed the horizon of the world. He is God's Son. He was human for thirty-three years, and He has always been God. Jesus is the sinner's Savior. He is the *centerpiece of civilization*. He stands in the solitude of Himself. He is august and unique. He is unparalleled and unprecedented. He is the loftiest idea in literature, the highest personality in philosophy, the supreme problem of higher criticism, and He is the fundamental doctrine of true theology. He is the core of spiritual religion. He is the superlative of everything good you choose to call Him! He is *the only one* to be called an *all-sufficient* Savior.

I long to know Him.

Jesus supplies strength to the weak; He is available for the tempted and the tried. He sympathizes and He saves. He strengthens and He sustains. He guards and He guides. He heals the sick and cleanses the tainted. He forgives sinners and discharges debtors. He delivers the captive and defends the feeble. He blesses the young and serves the unfortunate. He guards the aged, rewards the diligent, and purifies the meek.

He *needs and wants* to be our Lord!

Jesus is the key to knowledge, wellspring of wisdom, doorway to deliverance, pathway to peace, roadway to righteousness, highway to holiness, and the gateway to glory. He is the master of the mighty, captain of the conquerors, and the head of the heroes. He is the leader of the legislature, overseer of the overcomers, governor of governors and the Prince of Peace.

Have you ever truly accepted **His Lordship?**

His promise is sure and his light is matchless. His goodness is limitless and His mercy is everlasting. Jesus never changes! *His word and grace are sufficient.* His reign is righteousness. His yoke is easy and His burden is light. He desires to pick up whatever is wrong in your life and *fix it today!*

I wish I could describe Him to you, but He is indescribable. He is God! He is incomprehensible and *irresistible.* You can't get Him off your mind, and you can't get His blood off your hands. You can't outlive Him, and **you can't live without Him.** The heavens can't contain Him, let alone a man explain Him. The religious leaders of His day couldn't stand Him, and they realized they couldn't stop Him. No one could find any fault in Him. Herod couldn't kill Him, death couldn't handle Him, and the grave could not hold Him.

Jesus has always been and He will always be. He had no predecessor and there will be no successor. You can't impeach Him, and He is not going to resign. And His is the kingdom and the power and the glory forever and ever and ever, and if there is any time after forever, Jesus will reign supreme forevermore![1]

8

Only The King Can Give Us the Crown of Contentment

*My crown is called content; a crown that very few
have ever worn.*

William Shakespeare

Everyone, in some manner, strives for happiness, security, and contentment. My small glimpse of the world has revealed that most people seem to be struggling for the same things. For instance, friendship, family, love, religion, spiritual meaning, and/or happiness are commonly sought after by many. Striving for happiness is an especially common yearning of mankind. Does it seem to you also that the more we grasp for happiness, the more it seems to elude us?

I love the picture of the expanding universe. I envision God looking down at scientists and astronomers who are grasping for answers to how, where, and when the universe began. How in the world, or outside the world, is it sustained? Just when our so-called greatest minds think they have discovered the beginning or the end of the universe, the actual Alpha and Omega is somewhere beyond their understanding pulling the massive rug out from under their slippery man-made shoes. I wonder how many countless generations it will take to realize that the answer is not in figuring out how, where, or when. The Answer is Who!

How about us? Is our true *answer in the Who*, or are we grasping for happiness somewhere or somehow *in the world?* In your pursuit for happiness in the world do you feel like the scientists and astronomers mentioned above? I know I have and still do feel this way when I temporarily forget that there is true contentment only in *living in and for* the Who. Americans should be the happiest and most content individuals on the planet; and yet, the modern world can't seem to produce enough pills, plastic surgeons, and self-help related materials. Why is there so much unhappiness and discontentment in the world? If you happen to meet someone on a good day, or at the right time of a given day, they may be *temporarily happy*, but are they *truly content?*

Contentment means desiring no more than what one has, being satisfied. Are you and I truly content, or are we just happy sometimes? *Happiness is fleeting.* **Contentment endures in the down times and for the long run.**

A few years ago I watched one of the saddest things I had ever witnessed on television. It was an episode of "Extreme Makeover." I have heard that now there are shows for "extreme makeovers" not only on people, but also homes, gardens, garages, vehicles, kids, and spouses. One can say a lot of things about the money sources and creators in Hollywood, but you can't call them stupid. They have taken this festering sore in America called discontentment and capitalized on it in true Hollywood fashion. If I could get an extreme makeover, I could be more confident, secure, happy, or content. If I had a different look, body, home, or car, maybe I could wear *one of the world's* crowns of contentment. If only "The Nanny" could visit my house and change my kids, then we would have a happy family just like the Joneses on television. Maybe I could learn the secret of contentment from swapping places with a family that is so desperate they need to go on national television to try and find answers.

The extreme makeover I saw was of the human kind. It started out with a person feeling worthless because of the way she looked. "I believe I could be happier and more confident if I could totally change my appearance." Eight weeks and six major surgeries later, Joannie from Joplin, Missouri, had been totally reconstructed: new hair, forehead, eyes, nose, cheeks, teeth, neck, stomach, chest, butt, clothes, and of course, makeup tips. At the end of the show they ask this slightly overweight, robotic runway model how she liked her new look. Out of her recreated mouth came this monstrous distortion: "I am happy with my new look, but I have always believed it is what's on the *inside that really counts.*" What?! No you don't!!

This confounded lady from the "show-me-state" looked me and millions of other infatuated people directly in the eyes and lied, yes lied, while on, of all places, television. I had to stand up for the integrity of the extreme makeover. I yelled, "You are a liar, Joannie from Joplin." You don't really care about what's on the inside. If you did, you wouldn't have just subjected yourself to eight weeks of pain and suffering. Your kids wouldn't be asking, when they were reunited with you, "Where is Mommy?" And you wouldn't be secretly hoping that your husband (who looks more like me than Brad Pitt) would be the next lucky person to get an extreme discontentment makeover. I'm sure this marriage will be fine between Joannie (who now looks a bit like a robotic Angelina Jolie) and average Joe from Joplin because it is all about what is on the inside, *right?!*

My purpose is not to pick on Joe and Joannie from Joplin. The issue of discontentment, although not as extreme as the above situation, runs deeply throughout not just our society, but the entire race of mankind as well. Each of us struggle to some degree to be happy. And even though we may not define one of our main internal goals as contentment, the goal yearns deep inside us nonetheless. My conviction is that we human beings are not designed to be content within ourselves. Again, contentment equals desiring no more than what one has, being satisfied. There is always something different or something more to long for in the world. It seems that something or someone often tries to make us feel less than we are or could be. My belief is that one must surrender to something (Someone) greater than himself or herself. I am not talking about surrendering to a pill or to a plastic surgeon.

Granted, it would be easier to be "more content" without influences in the world trying to make us feel insecure, unworthy, ugly, or discontent. Evidently, there are all these millions of people out there who have it all together. They are secure and content with just who they are (remember, it is what is on the inside that really counts). Have you met any of these people? I haven't either, although for some odd reason most of the people I meet happen to be more attractive than me. Stop believing that those around you are happier or more content. A French Proverb states, "What makes us discontented with our condition is the absurdly exaggerated idea we have of the happiness of others."

The good news, or bad news, depending on how you view life, is that we are all hopelessly discontent in our own power. We could think of a whole book full of ideas about how elements in the world make us feel less content. The bottom line is that we cannot blame the world for our discontentment; *our contentment is out of the world's control.* We could live in a hermetically sealed mansion with every luxury at our fingertips and still be incapable of true contentment within our own power. Our selfish hearts just can't get enough of a bad thing. Could there be something greater that could rescue our selfish, discontented hearts? First John 3:20 gives hope to the hopeless: "In whatever our heart condemns us; for God is greater than our heart, and He knows all things."

How about allowing God to give us an *extreme contentment makeover?* Permit Him to inwardly transform us and set us apart from the world's standards and hollow philosophies. We can do it, or I should say, we can *allow it to be done to us.* We should love the three physically painless steps to this spiritual transformation.

1. Stop striving to be somebody for someone else.
2. Stop trying to find your purpose and mission in life; they have already been created.
3. Allow God to guide your life completely.

I realize these steps may seem to be lacking for practical application, but I am convinced that when we get sick enough of not being content, we will figure out what it means to allow God to completely guide. This is the truth of Proverbs 3:5: "Trust in the Lord with all your heart and do not lean on your own understanding."

We will also embrace the purpose and mission of life, which is to love the Lord your God with all your heart, and with all your soul, and with all your mind. If this purpose is set on our hearts, then the subsequent mission of loving our neighbor as ourself will flow naturally (Matthew 22:36–39). To test the success of the ultimate makeover from the world, ask yourself, "Is the somebody I am striving for on earth or in Heaven?"

Just as there are at least three steps to having an extreme makeover from the world and for God, I believe there are as many responses to the makeover as well. One response could be the following: "I don't want to allow God or anyone else to give me an extreme makeover away from the world's standards and hollow philosophies." Not even God can help someone with this response. The all-loving God allows His human creation to make the decision to live for themselves. The good and bad news for those who exercise their free will in this manner is that the world will be waiting to embrace them as they desperately grasp for happiness. As C.S Lewis so distinctly penned, "The one principle of *hell; I am my own.*"[1]

The second response may sound something like, "I do not need an extreme makeover from the world and for God. God is already a part of my life." The core problem with this response is that I am pretty sure that God desires all the parts of our lives. If you are content with giving God some parts of your life and you still don't see the need for an extreme spiritual makeover, then please read Matthew 13:44, Luke 9:57–62, 14:33, Acts 2: 42–47, 4:32–34, and 5:27–42. I believe God used these scriptures and others recently to help me accept the fact that He was only a part of my life. Accepting the spiritual reality that I needed an extreme makeover for God was the relatively easy part. *Acting upon the newly discovered convictions* proves itself most challenging each and every day.

Perhaps you are sitting somewhere on this spinning planet, wondering why someone or something is prompting you to desire a spiritual makeover. In the kingdom of this world there are worldly soldiers who are labeled the "few and the proud." In God's Kingdom the small number of spiritual warriors could be described as "the few and the humble." It takes an incredible depth of humility to admit that we need anything, especially an extreme spiritual makeover.

Perhaps you and I have admitted the desire and need for this radical step, but we don't know if we can live above the world's ever-changing standards. I don't know about you, but every time I've tried the latest answer in the world it didn't meet its promise. Maybe you have also made some type of radical attempt to be different within the religious structure in which you are involved. Perhaps it didn't seem complete. Or maybe the reception to your radical prompting was met with a lukewarm response from the people around you.

I believe God will always find a place for those who persevere to experience the extreme makeover that He longs to give us. Unlike the extreme makeovers of the world, where a person is partially transformed and then left to fend for themselves, God's makeovers totally transform our hearts. After the transformation, He is willing to stick around as long as we desire Him.

With God at the helm we need not be afraid of the unknown territories we will travel. He has already cleared the path for us. A safe, narrow road has been built for our pilgrimage. In choosing *His way* each of us can be one of the few and the humble, to wear the King's crown of contentment.

9

Life in Empty Hollow

Human Philosophy is a study that lets us be unhappy
more intelligently.

Anonymous

Human philosophies are so hollow. The ever-changing standards they create leave people so empty. My Father actually came up with this foundational truth many years ago. He spoke through the Apostle Paul, concerning true wisdom, in 1 Corinthians 1:18–20.

> For the word of the cross is to those who are perishing, foolishness, but to us who are being saved it is the power of God. For it is written, I will destroy the wisdom of the wise, and the cleverness of the clever I will set aside. Where is the wise man? Where is the scribe? Where is the debater of the age? Has not God made foolish the wisdom of the world?

Even though God is all-knowing, we still fail to listen to Him at times because the wisdom of the world sounds so good. You can say a lot of things about Satan. With confidence you can say that he is always wrong and he always has our worst interests at heart. One thing you can't say about the evil one is that he is stupid. He knows how to make the philosophies of the world sound right and *so very appealing.* That tricky little devil even makes some of them *sound godly.*

Not only do most of these philosophies not work, but they have caused thousands of years of confusion and heartache for societies and individuals. The emptiness these teachings have left in people's hearts alone could fill thousands of emotional Grand Canyons. Why is human philosophy such a personal and societal disaster? *It goes against the grain.* The real issue at hand is that God made the grain (His Word), and it is not good to go against the grain He made because this pits us against the Grain Maker.

This is an insight that wouldn't fill any canyon, grand or otherwise. Nonetheless, we may want to write this one down and refer to it at all those moments when life, for some strange reason, doesn't seem to be working. *Don't go against the Grain Maker!* It is oftentimes wise and absolutely necessary to go against the standards that secular societies have created, but it never works to live contrary to God's Word.

God had the Apostle Paul write this thought more succinctly in Colossians 2:8: "See to it that no one takes you captive through hollow and deceptive philosophy, which depends on human tradition and the basic principles of this world rather than on Christ" (NIV).

Let us compare a few of the countless disasters of human philosophy to the truth of God. Ironically first on the list of empty teachings of the world is "**Look out for #1.**" This principle makes perfect sense to *me.* Yes, take care of ourselves first. If we have any time left, we can try to help others. In fact, if everybody would do a better job fulfilling this first teaching, then we wouldn't have to waste our time taking care of anyone else. If everybody would just take care of their own business and focus on their own well-being, we would only be forgetting the most important Being—*God!*

I am far from a biblical scholar, but I believe the Bible does say somewhere (almost everywhere) that we are indeed designed to look out for #1. Unfortunately for the masses who have bought into the world's version of this principle, the #1 we were originally designed to look out for is God. Again, you may want to check with someone smarter than me on this, but I believe the original "looking-out-for order" went like this: look out for God first, others second, and if or when there is time leftover, look out for ourselves. The Scripture that comes to mind when I think of confirming this "look-out-for order" is—The Bible!

I could literally recite hundreds of verses from God's Word that completely counteract this one selfish, empty philosophy, that some really smart (in the world's eyes) and empty (in Heaven's eyes) person once thought he created. No, the being that this evil doctrine originates with is more diabolical than the worst of mankind. When followed, this empty teaching has led all of our neighbors in the history of time to *feel more* incomplete, discontent, selfish, and harassed in their spiritual gut.

Praise God that His Truth can fill the incredible void for anyone who is tired of looking out for ugly person #1. This void is so deep that only God could possibly fill it and keep filling it on a daily basis. Let's all admit that the greatest love affair we have in our life is usually with ourselves. Think about how the world stops when we are hungry, tired, sick, or when we *want* something, and we *need* it now! I believe God knew that mankind would choose the wrong #1, so He blessed us with numerous specific truths in His Word to combat this self-centered philosophy.

The next two really scary worldly philosophies usually sound like this: "*Just follow your heart*" and "*if it feels good, do it.*" Ordinarily, these two don't lead me toward God or loving other people. In fact, following my heart doesn't even work out well for me most of the time. Do you want to know what feels good to me, especially for immediate short term gratification? Comfort, selfishness, laziness, lust, greed, and a long list of other sins. In my selfish nature, it feels good and right momentarily when I get prideful with my wife. It feels right initially when I am justifying my impatience toward my children.

If I chose to follow that little organ called my heart, it would lead me to a life with little purpose or mission. I often tell my wife that if I don't feel like doing something, I probably need to do it. Sometimes I ask myself, "Bob, do you want to go serve a friend?" Typically, I answer, "No, I want to lie on the couch and read a book." In these cases, I am pretty sure that my heart is telling me to be selfish. I also know that it would feel more comfortable if I didn't have to get off the cushy couch, get dressed, get in the car, drive somewhere and help someone. So what do I need to do?

What would you do? The bigger question is what do we do most of the time? The biggest question may be, is there someone else we could follow who has a perfect heart of love, someone who always did the right thing, even though it usually didn't feel good. Jesus didn't always *obey* His *feelings*; however, He did always *obey* His *Father!* Notice Jesus' obedience in Matthew 26:38, 39: "Then He said to them, 'My soul is deeply grieved, to the point of death; remain here and keep watch with Me.' And He went a little beyond them, and fell on His face and prayed, saying, 'My Father, if it is possible, let this cup pass from Me; yet not as I will, but as Thou wilt.'"

If the #1 you are living for is you, I strongly recommend against the "follow your heart" and "if it feels good, do it" teachings that are so prevalent among the self-empowerment crowd. In my opinion, these popular philosophies will lead you to many empty destinations. If God is the one you desire to follow, then you need to run from this crowd like you just saw a big hungry lion, because the decisions these philosophies will oftentimes guide you into will devour your sense of personal righteousness and your conviction to follow the true biblical kingdom teachings of Jesus. Here are a few examples of what God's Word says about these deficient teachings that consist of being guided by feelings:

"The heart is more deceitful than all else and is desperately sick; who can understand it?" (Jeremiah 17:9).

"The inclination of man's heart is evil from his youth…" (Genesis 8:21, Holy Bible from the Ancient Eastern Text *"AET"*).

"Trust in the Lord with all your heart, and do not lean on your own understanding" (Proverbs 3:5, NKJV).

"For the Word of God is living and active. Sharper than any double-edged sword, it penetrates even to dividing soul and spirit, joints and marrow; it judges the thoughts and attitudes of the heart" (Hebrews 4:12, NIV).

Now let's examine another small sampling of God's view regarding the principle *"if it feels good, do it."* The following passages reveal His teaching clearly:

And He said to them all, "If any man will come after Me, let him deny himself, and take up his cross daily, and follow Me. For whosoever will save his life shall lose it: but whosoever will lose his life for My sake, the same shall save it. For what is a man advantaged, if he gains the whole world, and lose himself, or be cast away? For whosoever shall be ashamed of Me and of My words, of him shall the Son of Man be ashamed, when He shall come in His own glory and in His Father's, and of the holy angels" (Luke 9:23–26, KJV).

If then you have been raised up with Christ, keep seeking the things above, where Christ is, seated at the right hand of God. Set your mind on the things above, not on the things that are on earth. For you have died and your life is hidden with Christ in God (Colossians 3:1–3).

I will let God have the last word regarding the above two insufficient, worldly philosophies and move on to another equally popular tenet of the world. Sadly, this teaching and the ones previously discussed have crept in and made their home in the "Christian world" as well. The fourth principle in the worldly philosophy "hall of shame" proceeds as follows: *"Be strong and don't let anyone push you around."*

I do not know how to begin to address this mindset that the majority of proud pagans have adopted. Unfortunately, the overwhelming majority of professing Christians also live this unbiblical teaching, *when push comes to shove.* "Hey, I don't want my son to look for trouble, but if trouble comes to him, he needs to take care of business." Does that sound familiar? Probably because you have heard a professing Christian or even yourself say this.

What happened to the teachings of turn the other cheek, love your enemies, and live as peacemakers? See Matthew 5:9, 39, 44! In addition to these teachings, what about the example of *the teacher?* Jesus endured the most horrific verbal, mental, and physical abuse in history, and yet He *never* struck back.

I know from personal experience that these teachings of Jesus, even in "Christian" circles, are not popular. Forget "popular" because nothing truly godly will ever be popular with the majority of people. This teaching and call to a life of non-resistance is downright hard. If someone cuts us off in traffic, disrespects us or our spouse, hits us or our kids, and/or wrongs us in **any** other way, we are ABSOLUTELY not to strike back physically or, equally importantly, in our hearts. *The Answer* says, "**NEVER!**"

If you don't like this teaching which comes directly from the Sermon on the Mount and is indirectly laced throughout the entire New Testament, you may want to avoid learning about and modeling after the lives of Jesus, His apostles, and the unified church that lived this calling for the first 250 years, and more, after His resurrection. They let anyone and everyone verbally and physically push, beat, pillage, and even kill them and their families without striking back with fists or weapons. According to historical records, they strove with all of God's power, even in their hearts, not to strike back. The only one they stood up for was God!

When Jesus commanded them to "turn the other cheek" and to love your enemies, the apostles and the disciples of the early church actually obeyed. They seemed to believe that Jesus said what He meant and that He meant what He said. Do we believe this? I pray that I can obey my belief!

If you are not a professing Christian and just finished reading the above paragraph on a life of non-resistance, you are probably thinking that Jesus is in a nice land of dreams located somewhere outside of reality. I hear you loudly and clearly because I once thought that this idea of not resisting one's enemies was preposterous. I ask you, on behalf of all of us who are trying to fight with all His might to live as warriors of peace, to please live as peacefully as you can. I pray my fellow kingdom Christians don't cut you off in traffic and that our kids are good examples on the playground.

For all who profess to be Christians, I believe some **major examination** of the life and teachings of Jesus relating to His call to a life of non-resistance must be done and **acted upon!**

The fifth destructive worldly philosophy again focuses on the self: *"Pay yourself first."* This is exactly the philosophy the majority of people who *follow their heart* have been waiting for. This one has been around for awhile, but it has been capitalized on by a slew of idolized writers throughout societies who believe that financial wealth is one of the main keys to overall happiness. I have nothing against money, capitalistic societies, or companies making profits. I frankly don't care if a lot of people find a way to get rich quick or make a million in a minute. I simply think *God's Word directly opposes* this idea of paying ourselves first. Actually, I should care more about people accumulating excess wealth because the Bible says that it is extremely difficult for a rich man (one must work hard in America not to be rich) to enter the kingdom of heaven. Here is what else *the one* who gives us all of our ability to make all of our money says:

> Ye offer polluted bread upon mine altar; and ye say, wherein have we polluted Thee? In that ye say, the table of the Lord is contemptible. And if ye offer the blind for sacrifice, is it not evil? And if ye offer the lame and sick, is it not evil? Offer it now unto thy governor; will he be pleased with thee, or accept thy person? saith the Lord of hosts (Malachi 1:7, 8 KJV).

> Woe to you, scribes and Pharisees, hypocrites! For you pay tithe of mint and anise and cumin, and have neglected the weightier matters of the law: justice and mercy and faith. These you ought to have done, without leaving the others undone. (Matthew 23:23, NKJV).

How have we survived spiritually through the first five worldly philosophies? For the professing Christians who made it through these five unscathed, congratulations are in order. If you haven't succumbed to any or all of the above secular teachings, you have definitely risen above the worldly and religious masses. With that said, I would encourage you to make time to examine your life against the list more closely. These secular ways have been deeply ingrained in most of us since childhood. I know that fighting against them is a daily battle for me, and I have been intently examining the New Testament, the primitive church of Jesus, and my very soul for the past two years, especially regarding biblical separation from the world. Regardless of how deeply you choose to examine your convictions against the previous five human philosophies, the sixth philosophy must be addressed.

This man-made teaching is actually a *false religious doctrine*. I believe the sixth point in my list of worldly philosophies may have had its origin from the #666. **"Pray Jesus into your heart!"** I am open to discussing and considering many different teachings on a host of subjects. God's plan of salvation is not one of them! You bring me a teaching from the last few hundred years pertaining to child rearing, health, building a better mouse trap, etc., and I will examine it and use it if it seems to make sense. Many have tried to convince me of an American creation, of the past few hundred years, regarding another way to be saved eternally, a new way to have all my sins washed away, and a new way to receive the gift of God's Holy Spirit. This is one invitation I will *never accept!*

You had better believe that if "pray Jesus into my heart" was in the Bible, I would accept it wholeheartedly. I would not only have found it, but I would have embraced it. If God's plan of initial salvation and persevering to the end consisted of simply saying a prayer, asking Jesus to save me, I would say a hearty amen. Call me crazy, but my sinful heart would love foregoing Biblical repentance (2 Corinthians 7:10, 11), dying to myself daily (Luke 9:23) and complete surrender of my life to Christ (Luke 14:26).

Unfortunately for me, and even more unfortunately for those who have surrendered to the particular false teaching of praying Jesus into their heart, *this idea is not in the Bible.* We are talking about the **most serious matter any of us will ever consider,** *salvation! Read John 12:48!!*

The initial salvation process is not the end of a life in and with Christ, but it is an essential beginning. I plead with anyone who has sincerely adhered to this false religious teaching to go on an immediate personal retreat. Take only the New Testament, and try to forget everything you have ever been told or taught. Forget what Grandma did, a preacher says to do, or your church has always done. *For God's sake and yours* don't let this plea go unattended. At least read the Gospels and the book of Acts and be open to the plan of salvation God commanded at least 1750 years before the plan you may be adhering to today.

10

The World is an Evil Place and I Love it Too Much

I shall tell you a great secret my friend. Do not wait for the final judgment, it takes place everyday.

Author unknown

First, let's make sure we are on the same page about the world being evil. To demonstrate this truth, I have randomly chosen headlines from legitimate internet news sources. The following snapshot of our world was taken over a twenty-four-hour period. I am confident that you could find comparable or even worse examples of evil on any chosen day. These headlines may have been written to shock (unfortunately it takes more than the horrors listed below to shock most "civilized people" anymore); however, my intent is not to shock but rather to give a clearer basis for our need to separate and rise above this evil place.

"Boy, 8, arrested after attacking principal with wooden pole."

"Teen claiming to be vampire sentenced for molesting girl."

"New York sex offenders may be tracked by satellite."

"Boy accused of raping a 3 year old."

"Priest arrested for crucifying a nun."

"Man accused of over 300,000 molestations…arrested dozens of previous times."

"Child sacrifices in London."

"Sleeping pill use soars among youth."

"16,137 murders, 94,635 rapes per year in USA."

"Boy accused of raping neighbor's dog."

"World pedophile registry closer."

"Michael Jackson plans post trial, Neverland party."

"*Madonna* warns, all will go to hell if don't turn from wicked behavior!"

Mission control I think we have a problem!

The previous list should convince all of us that the world is an evil place. How can we escape the negative influences of the world? Don't we have to live in the world? How can we possibly rise above the *world's entanglements?* I have indirectly and directly given us The Answer, but in case we missed Him earlier let me share one of the most encouraging scriptures in God's Word:

> "These things I have spoken to you, that in Me you may have peace. In the world you will have tribulation, but have courage, I have conquered the world" (AED Translation).

With Jesus you and I can overcome the inherent evil in our society and the negative influences of the world around us. Now that is an overcomers group that I desire to join. It is encouraging to know that we can survive the bad elements of society, but what about the good things in the world? How do we overcome the good things in life, or

I should say, *how do we not get overcome by the good things in life?* Yes, you read that right.

In my opinion, the good things in life are much more dangerous than the blatantly bad things. For me specifically, the bad things aren't usually what Satan uses to drag me away from God. It is typically the *seemingly harmless* things like hobbies, activities, busyness, and striving for worldly success and security that I allow to drag me away. Even obviously good things like family, kids, and/or other relationships can pull us away from our relationship with Christ. All of these things, or any of them, can place God in second place. He does not *like or accept* finishing second in any person's race!

Even knowing the biblical truth that God must be first in my heart and life, I still must confess that there is a part of me that loves the world. However, a bigger part of me hates this world. I hate it because my Father in heaven is very serious about his children hating this world (1 John 2:15–17).

I hate that I am allured by the empty promises of worldly wealth and security. I hate the pressures of the world to perform and achieve "success." I hate that we have created a society where elementary school girls are going to tanning booths and going on diets. I hate that the world has created spiritual emptiness that worldly extreme makeovers try, but can't, fill. Ultimately, I hate that far too often some things of this world attract my mind and heart more than God does.

Hate is a powerful force. Jesus once used a form of the word hate when teaching what a true follower of His must do:

> "If anyone comes to me, and does not hate his own father and mother and wife and children and brothers and sisters, yes, and even his own life, he cannot be My disciple" (Luke 14:26).

Please don't hold back, Jesus, tell us what it really costs to follow and be with you. When I first read this passage nearly fifteen years ago, I thought Jesus was insane for telling me to hate family, hate myself, and hate my life! That doesn't mesh with the teachings in the self-helpnosis section of my local bookstore. What did Jesus mean? Simply put, a person must love Jesus **so much more** than all people and things in the world that it seems like he or she hates them in comparison. This is why I hate those parts of me that love the things of this world too much.

We were created to live in the world, but Jesus says we are not to be of the world just as He was not of the world (John 15:19, 17:14 ff.). We must be in the world to serve those in it. We must be in the world to help God in some small way to *save people from it*. But we **must** strive to be separate as we help serve and save!

Are you struggling with how being separate from the world can or should be applied to your life? I have been wrestling with its implication in my life for the past two years. Although there may not be a lot of black-and-white answers to how to follow Jesus' command, I believe God desires for us to intently examine biblical separation. The evil one who has been allowed to influence us in the world wants you and me to love anything or everything we can see, taste, touch and consume. So where do we begin when the negative influences are so pervasive all around us? How can we begin to limit the corruptive influences of the world that are slowly and subtly demoralizing us and our children? Let's begin with a few practical steps:

1. Turn off the television for a week.
2. Repeat step 1 for a month.
3. Repeat either step 1 or step 2 for a year.

Why did I choose television as the first form of corruption for elimination? Here are a few reasons taken from a recent internet article: I understand that these statistics could be slightly skewed for political reasons, but they are close enough to reality to illustrate my point.

- Percentage of households that possess at least one television: 99.
- Percentage of U.S. homes with three or more television sets: 66.
- Number of hours per day that television is on in an average U.S. home: 6 hours, 47 minutes.
- Percentage of Americans that regularly watch television while eating dinner: 66.
- Percentage of day care centers that use television during a typical day: 70.
- Percentage of parents that would like to limit their children's television watching: 73.
- Percentage of children ages four to six who, when asked to choose between watching television and spending time with their fathers, preferred television: 54.
- Hours per year the average American youth spends in school: 1,150 hours.
- Hours per year the average American youth watches television: 1,275 hours.
- Percentage of survey participants who said that television commercials aimed at children make them too materialistic: 92.

Hey, I am not naïve to think that this one simple positive action of turning off the television will completely stop the deluge of negative corruption we endure on a day-to-day and year-to-year basis. This action is a constructive beginning. I have been amazed at all the free time that has been made available from this one spiritually-prompted decision. It has given me *greater opportunities* to be *more devoted to God.*

What else in the world may be *alluring us away* from a deeper devotion to God? What thoughts, influences, or actions tempt us into a love affair with the world? Perhaps something in the fulfillment of your version of the American dream is separating you from God. Whether it is television, thoughts, influences, actions, or part of your American dream, turn it off. If we don't hate everything in the world in comparison to our loving and living for Christ, then we love something else too much.

11

We Can Wake Up from the American Dream

What you seek in vain for half your life one day you come full upon all the family at dinner. You seek it like a dream, and as soon as you find it you become its prey.

Henry David Thoreau

I am not sure how the majority of U.S. citizens truly define the attainment of the American Dream. The emphasis in the previous sentence is "truly define." How do you and I really define success? There are probably hundreds of ways the American dream has been defined in the past few centuries, but one component seems to be fairly consistent, that is the quest for money and material wealth. Few would argue that most Americans are intently focused on the almighty dollar. Whether we would be quick to admit it or not, the common belief is that the one who dies with the most toys wins (or is the one who is greatly admired). Those who live in a big house and drive a nice car are viewed as more successful. My question is, does an *attainment focused* American dream truly make one happy?

Let's consider the phrase "American dream." The words *American* and *dream* taken separately can be defined in a positive light: America is a country of many freedoms, and dreaming can be enjoyable and constructive. However, connecting dream with America can often become a nightmare. The American dream would not end up being a nightmare in most instances if attaining it only cost us money.

Unfortunately, some, if not most, of these *misguided* dreams/ nightmares cost people a majority of their time, intimate relationships, and, much too often, their principles. Stop and ask how, why, and what? How do I spend my time? Why don't I have more, or any, intimate relationships? What principles do I stand for now or did I *used to stand for* before I got caught up in my current ambitions?

The good news is that it is never too late to wake up from the dream, or at least choose to fulfill the dream, but only if it can be done with the proper priorities. There is nothing wrong with attaining and enjoying assets. It is okay to have a comfortable house. Most would say it is wise to plan for retirement. But I recently wondered if my heart and life were really focused on fulfilling *God's dreams or my own?* If my heart and life are mainly focused on my house, job, retirement, or the attainment of other forms of transitory security, then I truly am in the middle of a bad dream.

My two-year-old daughter Sonja recently told me she had a bad dream. Evidently, something big and dark was chasing her. I asked her what happened then. "I prayed and then I ran," she responded. I don't know if I could give better advice. Pray and run as fast as you can away from your current dream if it has become a nightmare for you and those you love. The big house with the even bigger mortgage payment is not worth *sacrificing* your marriage, family, friends, sanity, and, for heaven's sake, God!

Your kids don't care about the size of the house, a nicer or newer vehicle, expensive assets, or pre-paying for their college education. They care about spending time with their family. Our kids don't care about our version of the American dream. They desire us to be there to *experience their dreams*. Are our present goals and priorities taking us in the right direction? Take Sonja's advice. Pray and run if you are in a bad dream…a dream you probably don't want to come true.

These words of the fourth century B.C. Greek philosopher Plato are still relevant today: "We can easily forgive a child who is afraid of the dark. The real tragedy of life is when people are afraid of the light."[1] I spent so much of my life avoiding the light as I stumbled around this dark world pursuing dreams that cost me so much time, money, and most regrettably, close relationships. Deep down I desire and know I need to pursue God's dream so succinctly defined in Matthew 28:18–20.

> And Jesus came up to them and said, "All authority on heaven and on earth has been given to me. Therefore go and make disciples of all nations, baptizing them in the name of the Father and of the Son and of the Holy Spirit, and teaching them to obey everything I have commanded you. And surely I am with you always, to the very end of the age" (NIV).

Now, there is a dream you can and need to embrace.

The dream Jesus designed for us doesn't require assets. It should eliminate the stress that we have all felt while seeking after worldly security. Best of all, it requires us to have deep, meaningful relationships. To fulfill Jesus' dream, we must have a *deep, intimate* relationship with Him. We also need intimate relationships with those few who are willing to sacrifice their dreams for God's. This benefit alone compared to the oftentimes *shallow acquaintances* we maintain in the world is worth the cost associated with following Jesus' commands. The life of a true disciple of Christ who is wholeheartedly pursuing His dream comes with great costs. But **consider the cost** of living for idolatrous, worldly dreams. Misguided ambition, feelings of insecurity, and the loss of more intimate relationships is a cost no one needs to bear.

Pursue your American dream, and there is a good chance you will not reach it, leaving you feeling unfulfilled. Perhaps you attain the initial vision of your worldly aspirations, but then societal pressures or your own ever-changing desires change the dream. You may even attain the goal, only to wake up too late, and realize that it cost you almost everything God gave you to love. Pursue God's eternal dream, and He will allow you to live it with Him. C.S. Lewis wrote these spiritual sentiments more eloquently.

> "Aim at heaven and you will get earth thrown in.
> Aim at earth and you will get neither."[2]

I am not exactly sure what C.S. Lewis meant in a practical sense when he wrote about aiming at heaven and not at earth. Yet, I interpret his underlying meaning to be that we should take seriously the commands for God's children to be separate from the world, seeking after His kingdom first. As hard as professing Christians have tried (consciously or not) to escape from these commands, the truth still remains. There are two kingdoms on earth that desire our hearts' allegiance, and there is *only room for one kingdom per heart.* There is no escaping the specific call that is found throughout the pages of the New Testament. Each of us who profess to be His follower must *decide daily* for which kingdom we will truly live and die. You and I get to choose while alive; He gets to decide once we are dead.

Jesus' lordship in our lives is essential. An ever-deepening, *obedient love relationship* with Christ is vital. A *continual brokenness* at the foot of the cross must be our constant renewal of life. Along with all of these, each of us who professes to be committed to God must choose the kingdom that He has established. Our ambitions and dreams must be *radically different* from those striving for attainment in this lifetime. Examine the following biblical descriptions of God's unique calling for true followers of Christ:

Mark 8:34–36: "And he summoned the crowd with his disciples, and said to them, 'If anyone wishes to come after me, he must deny himself, and take up his cross and follow me. For whoever wishes to save his life will lose it, but whoever loses his life for my sake and the gospel's will save it. For what does it profit a man to gain the whole world, and forfeit his soul?'"

Luke 14:26: "'If anyone comes to me, and does not hate his own father and mother and wife and children and brothers and sisters, yes, and even his own life, he cannot be my disciple.'"

John 17:14–18, 18:36: "'I have given them your word; and the world has hated them, because they are not of the world, even as I am not of the world. I do not ask You to take them out of the world, but to keep them from the evil one. They are not of the world, even as I am not of the world. Sanctify them in the truth; Your word is truth. As you sent me into the world, I also have sent them into the world.
Jesus answered, my kingdom is not of this world. If my kingdom were of this world, then my servants would be fighting so that I would not be delivered up to the Jews; but as it is, my kingdom is not of this realm.'"

Acts 2:42–47: "They were continually devoting themselves to the apostles' teaching and to fellowship, to the breaking of bread and to prayer. Everyone kept feeling a sense of awe; and many wonders and signs were taking place through the apostles. And all those who had believed were together and had all things in common; and they began selling their property and possessions and were sharing them with all, as anyone might have need. Day by day continuing with one mind in the temple, and breaking bread from house to house, they were taking their meals together with gladness and sincerity of heart, praising God and having favor with all the people and the Lord was adding to their number day by day those who were being saved."

Romans 12:1, 2: "I urge you therefore, brethren, by the mercies of God, to present your bodies a living and holy sacrifice, acceptable to God, which is your spiritual service of worship. And do not be conformed to this world, but be transformed by the renewing of your mind, so that you may prove what the will of God is, that which is good and acceptable and perfect."

2 Corinthians 6:17–7:1: "Therefore, come out from their midst and be separate, says the Lord. And do not touch what is unclean; and I will welcome you. And I will be a father to you, and you shall be sons and daughters to Me, Says the Lord Almighty. Therefore, having these promises, beloved, let us cleanse ourselves from all defilement of flesh and spirit, perfecting holiness in the fear of God."

Colossians 3:1–3: "Therefore if you have been raised up with Christ, keep seeking the things above, where Christ is, seated at the right hand of God. Set your mind on the things above, not on the things that are on earth. For you have died and your life is hidden with Christ in God."

Hebrews 11:13–16: "All these died in faith, without receiving the promises, but having seen them and having welcomed them from a distance, and having confessed that they were strangers and exiles on the earth. For those who say such things make it clear that they are seeking a country of their own. And indeed if they had been thinking of that country from which they went out, they would have had opportunity to return."

James 1:27: "This is pure and undefiled religion in the sight of our God and Father, to visit orphans and widows in their distress, and to keep oneself unstained by the world."

James 4:4: "You adulteresses, do you not know that friendship with the world is hostility toward God? Therefore whoever wishes to be a friend of the world makes himself an enemy of God."

1 Peter 1:13–16: "Therefore, gird your minds for action, keep sober in spirit, fix your hope completely on the grace to be brought to you at the revelation of Jesus Christ. As obedient children, do not be conformed to the former lusts which were yours in your ignorance, but like the Holy One who called you, be holy yourselves also in all your behavior; because it is written, 'you shall be holy, for I am holy.'"

1 John 2:15–17: "Do not love the world nor the things in the world. If anyone loves the world, the love of the Father is not in him. For all that is in the world, the lust of the flesh and the lust of the eyes and the boastful pride of life, is not from the Father, but is from the world.

The world is passing away, and also its lusts, but the one who does the will of God abides forever."

Do the above scriptures look like your life? What about your church? Does your life and church not just sound like, but *look and live like* these scriptures? I am not just picking on you. I am struggling with the "look and live like" on both fronts. Please stop and take a few minutes to reread the above scriptures. These are just some of the passages that speak more directly regarding separation from the world. Most of the remainder of the New Testament has a spirit of the distinct and separate life of a biblical disciple of Jesus Christ.

I urge you to spend a few days, months, or even years if necessary examining what scriptures like these mean for your day-to-day life. Begin and end your study with the life and teachings of Jesus. If you feel that more examination is needed, I would encourage you to study the lives of some of Jesus' earliest disciples. I was greatly inspired and convicted while reading about the lives of the early followers found in a set of volumes entitled, *Ante-Nicene Fathers.*[3]

The early church chose to have nothing to do with the world's standards, ambitions, or dreams. Jesus and His earliest followers were convinced that two distinct kingdoms existed on earth; they believed that both kingdoms were battling side by side for the minds, hearts, and lives of people. They believed *only one* could be lived for and only one was worth dying for. The battle is still being waged today for the heart of every man and woman!

Each of us can wake up today from an American dream or any other dream outside of living for God and his kingdom. Do you have dreams for your life? Is that word "dream" throwing you a little bit? Do you not consider yourself much of a dreamer? Even so, you're not off the hook. Let me use another term I consider interchangeable with the word dream, i.e. *goal.* Whether you call them dreams or goals, just answer the question.

We must identify our dreams. Deeper still, what are our present realities? Our realities say much about our desires and dreams. In a chat room a voice of reason responded to these questions, as they relate to the book *The Great Gatsby*, with this message.

> "I dream of an American reality that aspires to spiritual achievement not darkly tied to a material phantom with a big house, big car and cold heart. A reality freed from the habits of a decadent age. A reality that embodies justice and peace; one in which my society and myself become a vehicle for the laws of God. May his Kingdom come and will be done."

Another voice responded to this dream of an American reality as follows.

> "I love the first line, 'I dream of an American reality.' I think that says it all for me. I would have to agree with what has already been said and say that I prefer the word reality to dream. I feel like too many people in this country are wrapped up in their own selves…going about their lives focused mainly on monetary and materialistic means to fulfill their desires. The American dream Gatsby wanted so badly is a world of plastic…it's fake and superficial. People are searching and searching for happiness in all the wrong places and oftentimes going as far as to hurt loved ones in their path. What is my American dream? My answer is God."

What is your American dream and reality? Is it *American or Godly* in nature? **Our lives will answer these questions** for us. In his book, *The Kingdom That Turned the World Upside Down*, David Bercot helps us examine how we daily prioritize the time God has given us:

Most American Christians will claim that the kingdom truly comes first in their lives. 'Sure, I have considerable treasure here on earth. But none of it means anything to me. My heart is on Jesus, not on these earthly treasures.' That's what most of us say, isn't it?

Perhaps that's what you yourself claim. And maybe it's the truth. But the heart of man is treacherous. That's why we all should do a thorough self-examination to determine what our hearts are really focused on. Here are some simple questions that may help you to do that.

1. The number of hours you spend each week in earning money, including commuting time.
2. The number of hours you devote each week to cleaning, maintaining, purchasing, and looking after material possessions.
3. The number of hours you devote each week to kingdom interests. I'm referring to activities such as witnessing, visiting the sick, feeding and clothing the poor, Bible study, prayer, fellowship, and other activities designed to take care of your family's spiritual needs or to further God's kingdom.

Now compare the number of hours you spend each week in kingdom interests with the amount of hours you spend each week to earn and take care of material things. Where does most of your time go? Obviously, some secular work is necessary to provide for the *necessities* of life. But do we really think we're going to be able to convince Jesus that we are working only for the necessities of life— not to maintain the comfortable American lifestyle?[4]

When I first read this portion of Mr. Bercot's book, I wanted to run off a cliff like the herd of pigs Jesus sent running. After a few days of torment I realized that this practical exercise actually pales in comparison to the constant call of Jesus. Among many scriptures, Luke 9:57–62 kept entering my heart.

And as they were going along the road, someone said to Him, "I will follow you wherever you go." And Jesus said to him, "The foxes have holes and the birds of the air have nests, but the Son of Man has nowhere to lay His head." And He said to another, "Follow Me." But he said, "Lord, permit me first to go and bury my father." But He said to him, "Allow the dead to bury their own dead; but as for you, go and proclaim everywhere the kingdom of God." Another also said, "I will follow You, Lord; but first permit me to say good-bye to those at home." But Jesus said to him, "No one, after putting his hand to the plow and looking back, is fit for the kingdom of God."

Take courage. If we truly desire that our reality and God's dream become one, He can guide us. His guidance is essential, but we will also need the help of others who have chosen to live a *separate* and completely committed life *for Christ*. Therein lies our success.

12

Success = Relationships

"Teacher, which is the great commandment in the Law?" He said to him, "You shall love the Lord your God with all your heart, and with all your soul, and with all your mind. This is the great and foremost commandment. The second is like it, you shall love your neighbor as yourself. On these two commandments depend the whole law and the Prophets."

Matthew 22:36–40

In life, family, church, and business how do we *really define success?* Take a moment to write out a brief definition of a successful life. Don't think too deeply about it; simply write down what comes flowing from your heart. What about a successful family? Try to define a successful employment situation. How should we measure a church's success? Please get "gut level honest" with these questions relating to your definition of success.

If the primary element of our model of success isn't relationships, then we are majoring in the minors. Success in life is measured and *judged* by our relationships, not by the things we attain or goals accomplished. Success in our families is determined by relationships, not the academic achievements of our children or the position our family holds in the community. Our place of employment should be judged based on the level of strong friendships, not simply on the level of economic success and professional development.

The evaluation of a successful church can ultimately be boiled down to two questions: (1) Do the members have a burning, growing, obedient love relationship with Christ? (2) Do the members lay down their lives for each other and the dying world around them? A successful church is not a place where my family is *comfortable* or a place that is *close* to where we live or a place with a *fun* children's ministry. These things don't necessarily signal an unsuccessful church, but they shouldn't be our measuring rod in choosing a place that is supposed to help get us Home.

Success in life, family, church, business, and final judgment will be judged in the spiritual framework of Matthew 22:36–40. The commandments of this passage are the two greatest for a reason! Everything of **eternal value** springs from these two commandments. If a person loves God with all his heart, soul and mind he will believe and obey Him when it comes to His plan of salvation and living a life under His Lordship. If God's perfect plan is followed, it will lead to a success that truly lives each day into eternity.

Here is a short list of ways I have measured success in the past: having a good-paying job, getting out of debt so that I could have more disposable income, experiencing a life of fun and adventure, being surrounded by like-minded people who would affirm my life choices, and having a solid retirement plan so that I would be able to live comfortably when I am old and uncomfortable. If you have one or some of these measuring rods of success, I urge you to get busy redefining your priorities. This reevaluation process is not a one-time event; it will probably be an ongoing challenge for all of us.

I am not opposed to money or material assets in principle. I recently started a small business from our home. I could literally make somewhere between nothing and a lot of money. I would prefer making toward the abundant end of the scale, but only if I could remain true and separate for God and only if I could *use the opportunity* of having an excess amount of money to help more people. Otherwise, I would prefer making nothing. If you have a goal of being a millionaire and can do it without losing your soul in the process, so be it. Forget the soul for a moment; if you can be a millionaire without *missing out* on someone else's life, then I wish you well within God's will. Keep in mind that one cannot serve God *and* money (Matthew 6:24).

The ultimate measuring rod of individual success in the end will be a true biblical relationship with God. The *ultimate measure* of success with regard to others will be the impact, or lack thereof, we had in helping them move into a relationship with God. I believe these eternal truths at a heart level. Living, and helping others to live, in the spirit of the greatest commandment is vital to a true walk with Christ. Like most of the commandments of Jesus, believing, and even understanding, is the easy part. For me, the hard part is having the humility and love to act on His commandments.

Two general questions will help us begin thinking about our current responses to the supreme commandments of Jesus. Is what I am doing *right now/today* building a relationship, first and foremost, with God? And like it, are these words and actions I am about to choose building relationships with others? Let me provide us with a few suggestions for the practical application of the two greatest commandments.

- Wake up at an hour that gives us ample time to tell and show God how we feel about Him.
- Choose the Bible over the newspaper with the morning coffee.
- Throughout the day talk with co-workers about God and not about other people.
- Be consistent in leaving work on time to go home to the important work of building your marriage and family.
- Once every few months tear up your family's weekend "to do" list and go to a neighbor's house and help them with their long list of chores.

- Sacrifice a really beautiful lawn and landscape to spend more time creating beautiful memories with those you love and others who need your love.

I wonder if you could think of an even more successful relationship-building plan?

I recommend getting away for a few days to sort out your new definition of success. Get away from your old surroundings, and try to find enough seclusion and peace to drive out any misguided priorities. Then *decide on the actions* you need to take to be successful for the remaining years you may have on earth. Actually, let me give you a shortcut. Figure out how to be successful eternally, and you will automatically be triumphant here on earth. God was gracious enough to arrange things like this for us.

Cry out for help from God. After He has set your mind at ease so you can see more clearly, consult with those you are responsible for and with. Then get some guidance from someone who has a radical relationship with Christ.

Along with trying to follow this biblical model, my wife and I usually make the "Ben Franklin T." I didn't pay close enough attention when my elementary teachers taught me about the life of Ben Franklin, but his graph for decision-making has saved me a lot of time, money, and many bad decisions. We will call this example the "New Success Franklin T." Mine would look something like this.

Of Increasing Importance	Of Diminishing Importance
Eternal happiness	Worldly happiness
Spend daily, intimate time, focused on God	Daily time focused on me
Separation of my heart and life for God	Desire to fit into the world's standards
Daily connection with family	Striving for no dysfunction in family
Live and help others live God's dream	Live and encourage others to live the American dream

After praying, seeking a lot of input, and wrestling with the "Franklin T of New Success," you should be filled with ideas and questions. Remember to keep the initial question in front of you as often as you can. Is what I am doing right now/today *building a relationship?* Now add this question. How can I involve someone else in my new plan for success? How could we involve others in our work, hobbies, and spiritual walk today? You will be amazed how many people will want to be a greater part of your new quest for relational success.

A greater focus on the two greatest commandments will not only change our lives, but it is waiting to change the people near our sphere of influence. This new success is *positively contagious* indeed. Our *new life* priorities will change our families and the families around us.

13

We Can Be Functional in a Dysfunctional Family

Happiness is having a large, loving, caring close-knit family that lives in another city.

George Burns

The title of this chapter is a comforting reality. Otherwise, we would all be in trouble. I am not just talking about some members in our families being dysfunctional. I am dysfunctional. You are dysfunctional. *Everyone is dysfunctional!* Since I don't know you yet and don't have time to talk about the dysfunction of everybody I do know, let me tell you about my dysfunctional life and family.

I grew up with two loving, wonderful parents. I thought then, and know now, that they are the best mom and dad in the world. They were also very dysfunctional; mainly with each other. They didn't get married with the intent of being dysfunctional. They set out not to do all the things their moms and sometimes-step dads did. You see my grandmas and sometimes-step grandpas grew up in dysfunction. In fact, I once did a family genealogy and was able to trace back the dysfunction to my very 1st Grandparents, Adam and Eve. Our original grandparents didn't have parents or siblings to blame, so Adam blamed Eve, and Eve blamed Satan for the dysfunction they created.

My mom and dad were dealt a pretty bad hand of dysfunction, and they picked up some cards of their own. My brother, sister, and I were dealt a lot less dysfunction than our parents, but we still received a decent amount. My siblings and I have chosen to hold some of the hand we were dealt, and we have decided to pick up some bad cards on our own. Sometimes in our marriages and child-rearing opportunities we kept some of the bad stuff and threw out some of the good stuff our parents taught us because we were so determined that we were not going to do everything like our parents did. Have you ever said that about your parents?

We all are dysfunctional! More than likely, you don't really accept that fact in your heart. We can accept this reality or continue on year after year subtly or blatantly blaming our parents, siblings, circumstances, boss, government, and anyone or anything else *but ourselves*. At some level, we have all placed blame on a family member for our shortcomings. I am going to let you in on a secret. Someone in your family is blaming you for either their or your overall family's dysfunction. Somebody needs to *stop the blame game*, and it might as well be you. We can rarely control the dysfunction, but we can always control our response to this verity of life.

Maybe my premise that you are dysfunctional is humbling. Let me share another humbling fact that also relates to all of us. We are in *control of very few things*. This fact was recently demonstrated to me by a friend who gave the following example. His premise was that we can't even control our phones. We don't know when they are going to ring, who is calling (if the caller really doesn't want us to know), or what the person is going to say. Along with the phone, we have very little control over most other things in life as well. We don't *ultimately* control things like our health, security, or future. Here is what we *can control—our responses* to whatever springs forth from life.

We can control our responses to family and any other dysfunction that individuals, culture, government, and even our own minds try to throw at us. Try responding in the following manner. Respond to dysfunction with *humility and love*. Some of the best advice my wife RoseMary and I ever received was, "If one of you **decides to be humble**, in any given situation, the conflict will begin to fade away." It takes two prideful people to fight! I wish this advice was as simple to follow as it sounds. For some reason, the person who has overlooked more of my dysfunction than anyone else is oftentimes the same person it is hardest to humble myself before. All I know is that when either RoseMary or I decide to be humble, regardless of the issue in question, the dysfunction subsides and the relationship is enriched.

When we make ourselves to be humble in a situation, it is so much easier to respond in love. The Bible says to speak the truth in love (Ephesians 4:25). Yes, even the dreaded truth, which most people don't naturally or really want to hear, can be more easily accepted when it comes from a humble spirit. Try it; what do you have to lose? Okay, maybe you will lose an argument. Actually, I have been amazed at the responses given to humility. It usually angers people at first because the last thing a prideful, argumentative person wants is resolution. But once they realize that their prideful anger is not going to defeat a humble, loving response, the relationship will slowly, or oftentimes quickly, begin to function more like you both want it to *deep down*.

In the spirit of humility, the following fact is a good reminder for all of us. The family we have, or will have someday, is, or will be, dysfunctional. RoseMary and I are trying with all of our hearts to pass on all the great things we learned from our parents. With equal determination, we are trying to avoid all the mistakes we have made and experienced. We pray, strive to live by the Bible (the perfect marriage and child-rearing handbook), and seek a lot of advice. I would consider us to be on the upper half of the parenting curve, and yet we in nine years of combined child-rearing have already made countless mistakes. We have committed thousands of sins against God and our kids despite our sincere attempts to raise our children in a godly manner. We have already messed up enough to fully justify our daughters someday visiting a family dysfunctional therapist.

We can't control exactly how our daughters will grow up. Will they become *true biblical disciples* of Christ, *or* will they be *devoured by worldliness?* Will their view of themselves and others be godly or worldly? Will they truly judge themselves and others based on inward or outward beauty? All we can do is strive to respond to them in humility and love, teach them in humility and love, and try our best to function as a family in humility and love. And when the inevitable dysfunction finds its way to our dinner table, I can only hope that my wife or I will aggressively escort it out of our home with humility and love.

On the flip side of the spiritual coin, when someone doesn't act in humility and love toward us, we still need to be in control of our responses. We can't completely control the amount of dysfunction in our families or the circumstances that life brings, so why not control what we can, i.e. our responses to the dysfunction. At the very least, your family will go from confrontational to *functional dysfunction.*

Maybe your family still won't be what you have always hoped for; they may not even care about building a more loving, functional family. Some in our families may not want to talk or listen to us at all. For all of us, regardless of our family and life circumstances, we always have One that longs to talk and listen to us. We always have One who truly cares.

14

Talk to Someone Who Cares

The hardest test I ever faced in my life was praying.

Malcolm X

Although I have come to disagree with the religious beliefs and the use of "justified" violence accepted by Malcolm X, at certain points in my life, I was very influenced by some of his words and by his courage. Nothing that I ever heard or read from him proved more true than his vulnerable admission that the hardest test he ever faced in his life was praying. I am convicted that this man, who faced so many tests in and from the world, realized praying was his toughest. I am even more convicted that prayer is *too often* not a test at all for me.

Reading the Bible can be difficult at times. Reading the Bible and doing exactly what it says is difficult most of the time. Praying, truly bearing my soul to God and believing the prayer is answered, even before I get up off my knees, is heart-wrenchingly arduous! Why should it be so hard to bear my soul to *the one* who loves me most? Why does it feel like at times I am not really taking the test?

The real trial was completed on Calvary! God chose His Son for me!! God allowed me to choose to be His son!!!

For anyone reading this book who doesn't believe in *one* greater than they are, I would suggest they try talking to someone on earth who cares. When that someone gets tired of listening or he becomes preoccupied with his own needs or can't meet your inward needs, you can try talking to yourself as a last resort. Begin by saying something like, "Self, I am tired of being unfulfilled, discontented, and dragged around by my ego. I am sick of trying to live by the world's corrupted, misguided standards."

Hopefully, you will end the conversation with yourself, realizing that you are looking for answers from the person who got you into the unfulfilled situation in the first place. Perhaps you have accepted a supposed answer from some source which I like to call "psychological babble." There are countless easy answers that fill our bookstores and airwaves. These so-called solutions usually avoid the source of the problem—us! They almost always lead us away from *the true answer.*

One of the worse dispensers of bad answers is found in television ads that recommend very serious medicines. When I was a kid, people went to the doctor to find out what was wrong with them. Now people watch television to find out what pills they need. A modern pharmaceutical commercial goes something like this.

> Do you ever get tired? Do you ever experience stress? Do you ever feel a bit down? If so, the _____ colored pill may be right for you. Ask your doctor about _____ or one of the other pills we manufacture. _____ is not for everyone. Side effects may include vomiting, hair loss, constipation, diarrhea, and blurred vision, (and the following additional effects they don't mention: less disposable income, higher insurance premiums for all other Americans, and an overwhelming sense of depression when the drug wears off)._____ should not be taken by nursing mothers, women who are pregnant, or women who plan to get pregnant (or those who are planning to spend time with pregnant women or children).

Wow, I think we may want to stay away from _____.

Why are prescription drugs advertised on television? Could it be that people are not talking enough with the *one* who really cares about them? At the end of the day, as the old saying goes, I recommend we all choose to talk with someone who always cares. In fact, I recommend these conversations not just at the end of the day but at the beginning and throughout the day as well. This decision has no side effects and has been proven to work, in real life trials, for centuries. God not only cares about your day, *He is the one* who defines what constitutes a good day.

Start talking with the One who cares, and don't stop talking until your *outlook changes.* If we talk long enough and listen intently, we will realize there is one common denominator in our stream of problems—us! That is okay. Just keep talking until you understand what and how you need to change. This uncovering is good news because it is a lot easier to change yourself than to change someone else. In most cases it is also easier to change yourself than to change a circumstance. Aren't you glad that **you are the problem?** Doesn't this fact seem like *good news* to you?

Now let's consider the more difficult challenge: accepting that you are the problem in whatever circumstance you face and letting God change you. Once you understand and accept that you are the root of the problem, you must allow God to direct your spiritual life change. Yes, we are back to talking with the one who cares. He not only cares but also has the *power to change* us. If you can accept His authority, He will change either you or your priorities, whichever *He deems necessary.* Accept, pray, change your priorities, and act, with the power He provides.

It seems like it should be so easy to accept, pray, alter priorities, and act, but in reality I many times turn to things in the world for my initial answers. Why don't I first turn to God? That question recently made me ask myself another question: Do I really believe in prayer?

When a situation arises in my life, do I turn to prayer first, or do I feel the need to do something (as if prayer is not doing anything!)?

The need of the hour is to pray in faith that God can change whatever situation you find yourself in, according to His will (Matthew 26:39), and then, and only then, do you need to do something. The bigger the issue or the more your heart wants to impose your will in a decision, the more time you need to invest in making sure His kingdom comes, His will be done. You must allow your prayers to become God's priorities. This also sounds simpler than it is because doing something is so much *easier and less intimate* than surrendering to God in prayer.

Are you beginning to see why prayer should be the hardest test you face each day? The test is offered to everyone each day and the answer is to always trust in God. As you embark on this daily test, I pray that the source of the answers is God and not your inward desires.

> The spiritual quality of prayer is determined not by its intensity but by its origin. In evaluating prayer we should inquire who is doing the praying—our determined hearts or the Holy Spirit? If the prayer originates with the Holy Spirit, then the wrestling can be beautiful and wonderful; but if we are the victims of our own overheated desires, our praying can be as carnal as any other act.[1]

As sincere and valiant as our cries to God may be and as hard as we try to pray on behalf of His Holy Spirit, the answers we receive will most often not make sense. His answers and priorities are directly opposed to most of the ways we have learned in the world. When the answers don't make sense, pray with all your might and seek God's wisdom to trust in His uncommon sense.

15

Trust in God's Uncommon Sense

Before God we are equally wise and equally foolish.

Albert Einstein

The world's common sense almost always leads us astray. At the very least, it doesn't typically work in a spiritual or eternal context. Even though much of the world's common sense is a proven disaster, and God has never been wrong, it is still difficult to trust in His "uncommon" sense. Wouldn't it seem to be wise to completely and wholeheartedly trust in something that has never been wrong? Wouldn't you invest your money in a stock that had a return of 100% every year for thousands of years?

It becomes difficult to truly trust and obey God's uncommon ways because in doing so, one often must go directly against the world's teachings. That person will be drastically different from the majority of people around them. Strictly obeying God's Word will oftentimes make us unpopular or unpatriotic in our society. I know from personal experience that making decisions that have caused me to stand out is uncomfortable. Don't we all have a *yearning to fit in?*

Obeying the entirety of God's Word does not combine well with the world's obsession with tolerance. It hardly ever fits in with the politically-correct, open-minded, you're-okay-I'm-okay society that we are currently a part of. In God's plan there are definite winners and losers. He calls people out of the world and into a kingdom that is distinct from the kingdom which dominates society today. The ways of God displayed through the life and teachings of Jesus are downright offensive. They are offensive to non-believers as well as to most professing Christians, who tolerate and eventually accept and live by the world's standards.

The way of God, preached and lived through Jesus, is so radical and *controversial* that it usually has no chance of really prospering in any type of worldly society, even a so-called Christian one. The teachings of Jesus such as the Sermon on the Mount and the writings from Paul, John, Peter, and James that go against our society's demand for tolerance and political correctness are rarely preached in American churches. Usually, they are mentioned only in a theoretical setting. *The Sermon on the Mount is not a theory* Jesus merely wanted discussed. *It is a teaching to be obeyed;* **it is a life to live!** We are not called to make sense of it as it relates to the moral standards of American society. *We are called to live it in opposition to society!*

Here is an abbreviated list of biblical teachings that aren't received well by most non-Christians, and even "Christian" people of the world.

- Your life should contain not even a hint of sexual immorality (cf. Matthew 5:27–29, Ephesians 5:3–5).

- Marriage consists of one man and one woman and should happen only one time (cf. 1 Corinthians 7:10, 11 Mark 10:11, 12).

- Love and pray for our enemies (cf. Matthew 5:38–44, Luke 23:34).

- Consider persecution a blessing (cf. Matthew 5:11, 12, 1 Peter 4:12–14).

- Do not gossip (cf. Romans 1:28–32, Proverbs 20:19).

- Men should lead and love their wives (cf. Ephesians 5:25, Colossians 3:19).

- A woman should submit to her husband (cf. Ephesians 5:22–24, 1 Corinthians 11:3).

I could go on for a very long time because in almost every area, God has a different standard than the one my humanistic instincts dictates (1 Corinthians 1:18–25). I don't know you personally, but I bet you think more like me than you think like God. We would probably agree that most of God's teachings and plans for mankind don't seem to make sense, especially when we try to fit them into the ways of the secular world. Trying to fit a perfect, all-loving, all-knowing, selfless being into an imperfect, little-loving, little-knowing, selfish people doesn't work well.

God gives us the choice of either trusting in His Word or trusting in our biased reasoning. Again, God is always right, and the source of our common sense is usually wrong. Typically, our decisions are derived from selfish desires or worldly learning. Logically, it doesn't seem like a very difficult choice, but the overwhelming majority of people adheres to and obeys the ways of the world and not God's Word.

In my experience, most religious people don't follow God's way of salvation. A belief leading to repentance, baptism, and Lordship are rarely followed. Repentance and baptism should be the easy part. Striving daily to live a separate and surrendered life for Christ is where the battle for Lordship is waged.

My educated spiritual guess would be that about one percent of Americans survive the three "S's" from above (salvation, separate and surrendered). The first "S," salvation, eliminates an estimated ninety percent of the people, and the other two "S's" eliminate the other nine percent. I use the above percentages to make a point. Obviously, I don't know what is truly in anyone's mind and heart (I am still trying to figure out my own mind and heart), but I am confident that the number of people who truly believe and obey in the commands of God is much closer to the one percent side of the scale. The problem is that close to ninety-nine percent of the people in America would probably label themselves as the one percent *simply because they believe.* Many people believe they are "Christians" just because they are born into a "Christian Nation."

The labeling of the United States as a "Christian Nation" and then deducing that all people born in this nation are therefore Christians is not part of God's uncommon sense. In fact, it falls under the category of nonsense. A person's nation cannot make a decision for him or her to be a true follower of Christ, nor can someone's family or church make this decision on his or her behalf. No, you and I must make the decision to totally believe in, and wholeheartedly obey, God's Word.

For most people, the discovery of this truth will mean an almost total mind, heart, and life makeover. For those who choose God's makeover let me go ahead and call you some names and labels to help you make the transition toward the one percent: closed-minded, politically-incorrect, backward-thinking, Neanderthal. Take courage in the fact that Jesus, His apostles, and the disciples until the early fourth century *chose* to be social, political, and spiritual outcasts. Are you ready to sign up?

I have already signed up, but I believe it is time for me to re-commit to a lifetime tour of duty. God has allowed me to take many tests since He saved me in the waters of baptism. During the past year or so I believe He has been trying to give me a very specific assignment: to be separate from the world. This test has proven much harder than the initial gift of salvation. It is challenging me to the core of my being, demanding an answer to the following question: am I willing to be a completely surrendered, social outcast for my Lord (1 Corinthians 4:9–13)? Another "S" keeps trying to get between me and my Daddy in heaven—self.

I must keep reminding myself that *self* is the one who almost always gets me in trouble. Down deep I don't trust "self." My selfish inclinations have gotten me in some real predicaments, when I chose to trust in them rather than trusting in God's selfless dispositions. Following self **feels** so right most of the time. It seems to make more sense within *my worldview.* Let me give you an extreme, but practical, biblical scenario to illustrate how self seems to make more sense.

I recently found myself in a discussion regarding the Bible's position on divorce. "What if" is usually how a discussion begins as we try to find a loophole around God's Word. "Bob, what if a husband in our church began physically abusing his wife? Should we advise her to stay with him or leave?" I could find nothing in the Scriptures saying she couldn't leave for safer ground. The next question was, "What if the husband moved away, leaving her with the three kids, and sometime later the wife met a good man in church and wanted to get married?" He even referred to an actual woman from our church named Carrie, to make it emotionally harder for me to stick to whatever uncommon sense I may find.

According to the Bible as I understand it, she can leave that situation and doesn't have to return to the husband, but she cannot divorce him or remarry. WOW! Does it really say that? You can check it out yourself if you want to be even more alarmed (I Corinthians 7:10, 11 Matthew 5:32). These hard-line teachings don't *feel right.* The implications don't seem *fair.* Who am I to tell Carrie or anyone else what to do? Fortunately, I don't have to tell anyone what he or she has to do, because the Bible has already told everybody what to do. This is so challenging and downright gut wrenching for anyone with an ounce of compassion.

In Luke 18:18–30, the Apostle Peter and some other followers watched a very religious man walk away sad because there was *one thing* he was unwilling to do for Jesus. Someone in the crowd asked, who then could possibly be saved? (This guy seemed to have everything going for him from a religious and worldly position). Jesus reminded them that with God all things are possible. "We have left everything and followed you," Peter replied. Jesus convicted and comforted them with these words:

> "Truly I say to you, there is no one who has left house or wife or brothers or parents or children, for the sake of the kingdom of God, who shall not receive many times as much at this time and in the age to come, eternal life."

The path of *most resistance* was only designed for those who would be willing to give up everything on earth so that Jesus could truly be their Lord. Charles Swindol expressed the above belief in the following way: "God does not dispense strength and encouragement like a druggist fills your prescription. The Lord doesn't promise to give us something to take so we can handle our weary moments. He promises us Himself. That is all. And that is enough."[1]

Is God enough? If He chose to strip us of everything, or even just some of our treasured worldly things, would He be enough? Who, that you and I would trust, ever said it was going to be easy? If it was easy, more than a mere fraction of preachers would have the courage to actually preach the biblical teachings regarding divorce and other socially sentimental topics. If more than a mere fraction of people were willing to follow Jesus and His Word, *without compromise*, then more preachers may be emboldened to preach about controversial issues.

Just this one biblical topic affects so many in our society, where divorce has become another quick fix with very little moral ramifications. I haven't researched the following comparison, but there seem to be as many advertisements for divorce as there are for a painless bankruptcy, instant relief from depression, a fast-track to getting rich, or a legal group who can win a big lawsuit for us. It all sounds so easy, especially if we don't get tripped up in any moral implications. Don't we deserve to be with someone who appreciates us more? Don't we deserve to be happy? Don't we deserve to be debt-free? Don't we deserve to be rich? No, No, No, No! **He never** said it was going to be easy.

I keep reminding myself again and again and again that God has never been wrong; that He created and sustains everything; that He is all-knowing, all-powerful and perfectly righteous. Even after recognizing all the above eternal truths, I can still struggle and waver in trusting His uncommon sense!

I encourage you to experience *God's way*. Don't simply try to intellectually grasp how His ways are radically different. God's ways are created to be acted upon. Every time I have trusted His way, through wholehearted obedience, it has always *eventually* made perfect sense. Richard David Bach writes in his book, *Jonathan Seagull*, "Sometimes when learning comes before experience it doesn't make sense right away."[2] More importantly, the Book of John, chapter 8, verses 31 and 32 says,

> "To the Jews who had believed Him, Jesus said, 'If you hold
> to My teaching, you are really My disciples. Then you will
> know the truth, and the truth will set you free'" (NIV).

I have a tendency to feel the need to understand the truth before I commit to obeying it. In these instances, I am forgetting one very important eternal truth. *God is smarter than we are.* I know that few people would verbally claim to be smarter than God, but that is exactly what we are doing when we do not trust and obey His Word. When we give in to our feelings and sense of fairness in situations like the one in which Carrie divorces her physically abusive husband, we are *in essence saying* that we have a better solution than God does.

We must decide for ourselves which path we will travel: the wide, winding road of the ever-changing moral and political standards of the world or the narrow, never-changing way of God. We can choose to be politically and in many other ways correct with the world, or we can decide to live spiritually content in and for Christ.

16

Politically Content

You begin saving the world by saving one person at a time; all else is grandiose romanticism or politics.

Charles Bukowski

Politics is *not the solution!* I am not going to spend much time bashing politicians or the political process, because there is not a shortage of people in the media slamming one or the other. I do believe that the majority of Americans are heated close to the boiling point by groups who try to force their politically correct agendas. Most people are also sick of our so-called leaders bickering for power, while America experiences a moral decay like never before. It appears that small numbers of special interest groups and handfuls of politicians, outside the mindset of most Americans, exert a lot of pressure and power on the democratic process.

I am going to talk about being correct politically, as *opposed* to being politically correct. First, let me confess that I am fascinated by the political process, especially presidential politics. In my thirty years of adult life (some claim that I haven't been an adult quite that long) I have been liberal, moderate, and conservative. A friend asked me a few months ago if he should be politically liberal, moderate, or conservative. My answer was "No!"

If you feel an innate need to be political, then choose to be politically incorrect with a loving heart. I would strongly recommend you choose a third and rarely traveled path: decide to be politically content. Contentment is the theme of this book, and it can be applied to the political process as well. How can a person be content politically? How can we keep our hearts from being poisoned by politically correct pressures? How can we not get swept up into a thirst for power as we seek it on the coat tails of politicians or political parties?

First, we must realize that there are no permanent solutions in political answers. **There are no permanent solutions in political answers!** Once I came to terms with this fact, I was able to step out of the contentious process without reservation. I was able to *focus more time and positive energy* helping point people toward the things that God really cares about. William F. Buckley wrote these timeless sentiments regarding politics: "I mean to live my life an obedient man, but obedient to God; never to the authority of political truths arrived at yesterday at the voting booth."[1]

When I ran with the liberal crowd, I could never reconcile with the conservative views that seemed to make more sense. There were *major inconsistencies* with both political sides. For example, my liberal friends were usually against the death penalty and war, but they were pro abortion. Huh? I would talk to a conservative and he would usually support the death penalty and war but was almost always against abortion. Huh? I found that moderates were usually swayed by either the crowd they were around or a persuasive politician. Huh? Jesus is very clear about a life of *complete nonviolence.* It seems to me that what was a black-and-white spiritual issue to Jesus is a debatable political issue in our modern-day society.

As the number of irreconcilable issues grew with my liberal friends, I found myself more inclined to conservative principles. Nonetheless, I still disagreed with many issues on the right side of the aisle. So I went to the middle of the aisle for awhile, picking and choosing what I felt was the correct position on each issue. I tried to convince the right that some of the answers on the left were correct, while attempting to convince the left that it was okay to be right sometimes (some pun intended). What I concluded in the end of that stage of life was that most people on both sides were too afraid to let go of their political positions. The discussions usually became emotionally charged and at times downright uncivil.

I realized one day that even if I was able to persuade either side toward a middle ground, or one side to the other side, regarding one of the hundreds of issues of contention in the political process, it would not *really matter.* At that point of clarity, I began to become more at peace with the thought of staying outside the political process. I unequivocally realized that helping myself and others become more like Christ instead of more like a political party would cause real change in the world. I was momentarily ashamed at how I had allowed myself to get so involved in a process of conflict and had *lost my focus on the true source of contentment.*

Then one day something, or Someone, tripped me at a bookstore causing me to fall into the following words of wisdom: "I do not believe in political movements. I believe in personal movement, that movement of soul when a man who looks at himself is so ashamed that he tries to make some sort of change within himself, not on the outside."[2]

Today when people try to label me politically, it is usually incorrect. I am definitely politically incorrect as defined by most in the mainstream media and some powerful special interest groups. The majority of these powerful individuals and groups may be labeled politically correct, but in my view they are usually *morally incorrect.*

I am going to keep *campaigning for Jesus!* He shunned politics and He was never incorrect. Jesus refused to be involved with the so-called solutions that politics promised. John 6:15 confirms his conviction:

"Jesus therefore perceiving that they were intending to come and take him by force, to make Him king, withdrew again to the mountain by Himself alone."

The twelve apostles deliberately avoided political affairs. The next seventy-two disciples Jesus sent out had nothing to do with the partisan process. For approximately three hundred years after the resurrection of Jesus, those who left behind everything to follow Him chose to leave the political infighting to those of the world. An elder in the church around the year A.D. 200, as a matter of fact, wrote, "The Caesars too would have believed on Christ, if either the Caesars had not been necessary for the world, or if Christians *could have been* Caesars."[3] Near the same time frame the following unified belief was voiced regarding a Christian's involvement in politics:

"Nor is there anything more *entirely foreign* to us than affairs of state."[4]

My biblical conviction is that we should choose to be politically content by staying out of the petty political process. It is admirable to seek ways to improve people's lives, but politics will not change an individual or group internally or, most importantly, *eternally*. There are no ultimate solutions in politics! If you are compelled to be political as you are fulfilling your duties for Christ, then by all means necessary, be politically incorrect. To maintain our integrity in the process, we must display and truly have a loving heart, as outside and inside forces move us to this state of political incorrectness.

Let us always remember that if we really want to give people solutions and help them be content, this will not happen by converting them to a political party. We must convert people to the solution and *source of contentment.*

17

Jesus Doesn't Need to Be Converted

I believe that unarmed truth and unconditional love will have the final word in reality.

Martin Luther King Jr.

Mankind (myself included) has subtly converted Jesus and His church over the past 1700 years. For those reading this book who do not profess to be Christians, you may benefit from a little biblical history. **Jesus did not come to earth to be converted.** Conversion is defined as a change in which one adopts a new religion, faith, or belief. Have we Christians converted Jesus by altering His life and teachings to fit our twenty-first century society?

In the mid-twentieth century, evangelist and writer A.W. Tozer wrote this disturbing depiction regarding the state of Christianity:

> The new Christian no longer wants to be truly good or saintly or virtuous. He or she wants to be happy and free, to have peace of mind and, above all, wants to enjoy the thrills of religion without any of its peril. He or she brings to the New Testament a paganized concept of the Christian way and makes the scriptures say what he or she wants them to say. And this the new Christian does,

oddly enough, while at the same time protesting that he or she is in true lineal descent from the apostles and a true son or daughter of their revolution. This person's spiritual models are not holy men but ball players, fighting men from the prize ring and sentimental but unregenerate stars of anything but heavenly firmament.[1]

Fortunately for this fiery man of God, he is not alive today to see the downward spiral our society and churches have taken since penning his thoughts just over fifty years ago.

The Lord Jesus has never and *will never need a conversion.* We do! My life and this book need to be altered. His life and Book does not need to be altered! Granted, we may feel Jesus needs to be converted if we don't want Him turning our entire lives upside down. Jesus is without question the most radical man who ever lived. His calling of complete surrender and obedience seem crazy to someone with a worldly mindset. He spoke of things nearly two thousand years ago that are so politically and socially charged in most first-world cultures today that very few in those societies are *willing* to read His Word and *do exactly* what it says.

A heart and a life devoted to service and sacrifice, separated from the allurements in the world is more than most people are willing to give. Calling people to this life, and *unapologetically* teaching people to adhere to a lifestyle of nonviolence, devotion to serving the poor, and living a life of purity is more than most church leaders can afford to do.

Trying to live for Christ and His *kingdom teachings* has proven extremely difficult and *isolating* for me. Adhering to His doctrine of initial salvation has its share of worldly costs. Reading and obeying some of the teachings of Jesus has its elements of sacrifice. Yet truly living for only Jesus and His kingdom is nearly impossible. However, I know it's not impossible because hundreds of thousands believed in Jesus and completely devoted their lives to Him for a few hundred years after He vanished in the clouds.

I believe there have been devoted individuals over the centuries who have done the same. In my estimation there have also been a handful of movements since the fourth century A.D. which consisted of people who were willing to live and die by the New Testament teachings. I am not aware of any groups in the past few hundred years that have adhered to both the doctrine of salvation and lifestyle by which the early church so valiantly lived.

There are probably dozens, if not hundreds, of ways most professing Christian's beliefs don't line up with the New Testament and the Apostolic Church. Although it may seem a daunting task, there is some good news in allowing ourselves or encouraging our churches to be turned upside down. I believe many have been *misguided doctrinally.* In some cases changing to a right doctrine doesn't add more time commitments to our lives. Sometimes it is simply a matter of changing our thinking and then teaching differently. For many individuals and churches baptism would be a specific example of this.

On the other hand, many times the changes affect our lives in very direct ways. I have discovered that it is very challenging to take a strong stand for many of the lifestyle related issues on which the New Testament teaches. The challenge is twofold:

1. It is both arduous and inconvenient personally to make the lifestyle changes.
2. Following socially controversial parts of the Bible is not readily accepted in secular society, or in many cases, "Christian circles."

I am not talking about trying to be a perfect disciple or become the perfect church. I am simply trying to focus us on the core issues of doctrine and lifestyle set forth in the Scriptures that many, if not most, individuals and groups have *either* altered or completely ignored.

The following are a few of many examples of doctrinal and lifestyle issues that I've been *compelled to reexamine* in my life. My fear is that most churches are not preaching and living at least some of these biblical teachings. Each of us will have to decide if, or how, we are going to change our individual beliefs and actions to coincide with the Scriptures. Some of these topics have been mentioned in previous chapters, but I believe they are so foreign to most of us that they deserve more lengthy discussion. For each topic, I will quote two out of the many related Scriptures and one excerpt from a primitive church writing.

Baptism

Acts 2:36–38: "'Therefore let all the house of Israel know for certain that God has made Him both Lord and Christ—this Jesus whom you crucified.' Now when they heard this, they were pierced to the heart, and said to Peter and the rest of the apostles, 'Brethren, what shall we do?' And Peter said to them, 'Repent, and let each of you be baptized in the name of Jesus Christ for the forgiveness of your sins; and you shall receive the gift of the Holy Spirit.'"

1 Peter 3:21: "And corresponding to that, baptism now saves you—not the removal of dirt from the flesh, but an appeal to God for a good conscience—through the resurrection of Jesus Christ."

"Before a man bears the name of the Son of God, he is dead. But when he receives the seal, he lays aside his deadness and obtains life. The seal, then, is the water. They descend into the water dead, and they arise alive."[2] Hermas, A.D. 150

As was recorded earlier in this book, the word baptism comes from the Greek word, "Baptidzo," meaning "immerse." It is the only *word ever used* in the New Testament in reference to water baptism. But the issue with baptism runs deeper than the mode of water. The problem in "Christian" circles that participate in some form of baptism is the timing and understanding of the event. Baptism is not a ceremony to have after one is saved. It is not an outward sign of an inward grace. To the truly repentant heart the water is where one receives the forgiveness of sins. As Peter says in *1 Peter 3:21, this water saves us: we are still dead before we descend into the water.*

The idea that salvation comes by merely accepting Jesus into one's heart is **not found in the Bible!** It began in the latter part of the 1600's. Martin Luther's teachings add the word "alone" to Ephesians 2:8 to justify his own misguided doctrines: "For by grace you have been saved through faith [alone]; and that not of yourselves, it is the gift of God" (NIV). No one is arguing that it is God's grace that allows us to even have a chance of responding to His plan. But the Apostle Paul, in other biblical writings, wrote very clearly about baptism being an essential element of salvation.

Praying Jesus into your heart is **not in the Bible!** This false doctrine established its foothold in the early 1800's in rural American revivals. Being baptized for the forgiveness of your sins and to receive the gift of the Holy Spirit is **in the Bible!** A person is not saved until their sins are forgiven (Isaiah 59:1, 2). The Apostle Peter set forth the true doctrine of salvation in Acts 2:22–38. I believe I am going to *choose God's Word* over Martin Luther and some fiery preachers of the early 1800's.

What will you choose? What have you chosen up to this point of your life? If you don't agree with the above Scriptures or historical information, will you invest the time to prove that "accepting" or "praying Jesus into your heart" are Scriptural? I believe the investment is worth it since salvation and eternal life are in question!

Now on to other important issues not relating so directly to *initial* salvation.

Nonviolence

Matthew 5:38–40: "'You have heard it said an eye for an eye and a tooth for a tooth. But I say to you, do not resist him who is evil; but whoever slaps you on your right cheek, turn to him the other also. And if anyone wants to sue you, and take your shirt, let him have your coat also.'"

Romans 12:19–21: "Never take your own revenge, beloved, but leave room for the wrath of God, for it is written, 'Vengeance is Mine, I will repay,' says the Lord. But if your enemy is hungry, feed him, and if he is thirsty, give him a drink; for in doing so you will heap burning coals upon his head. Do not be overcome by evil, but overcome evil with good."

"Above all else, Christians are not allowed to use violence to correct the delinquencies of sin" (Clement of Alexandria, A.D.195).[3]

Nonviolence should be our way of life because it was the way of Jesus, who is *the life*. The apostles and the people of the primitive church were arguably some of the bravest who ever walked the earth. It wasn't in cowardice that they chose not to defend their property, families, or themselves against the violence of the world. Nonviolence and nonresistance were *not optional* to Jesus and His warriors of peace.

Separation from the World

James 1:27: "This is pure and undefiled religion in the sight of our God and Father, to visit orphans and widows in their distress, and to keep oneself unstained by the world."

1 John 2:15–17: "Do not love the world, nor the things of the world. If anyone loves the world the love of the Father is not in him. For all that is in the world, the lust of the flesh and the lust of the eyes and the boastful pride of life, is not from the Father, but is from the world. And the world is passing away, and also its lusts; but the one who does the will of God abides forever."

"We who are trusting that we shall reign with Christ, ought to be dead to the world. For you can neither desire martyrdom till you have first hated the world, nor attain to God's reward unless you have loved Christ. And he who loves Christ does not love the world. For Christ was given up by the world, even as the world also was given up by Christ; as it is written, 'the world is crucified unto me, and I unto the world.' The world has been an object of affection to none whom the Lord has not previously condemned; nor could he enjoy eternal salvation who has gloried in the life of the world. That is the very voice of Christ, who says: He that loveth his life in this world, shall lose it in the world to come; but he that hateth his life in this world, shall find it in the world to come" (Treatise on the Glory of Martyrdom, A.D. 255).[4]

Jesus, the apostles, and their beautiful band of brothers who made up the primitive church chose to think, live, and die differently from those in the world around them. They refused to adopt the various and ever-changing social standards of their worldly sojourners. The choices of the early followers of Jesus give me the encouragement to believe that it can be done by a carnal man like me.

Purity/Modesty

Matthew 5:28, 29: "'But I say to you, that everyone who looks on a woman to lust for her has committed adultery with her already in his heart. And if your right eye makes you stumble, tear it out, and throw it from you; for it is better for you that one of the parts of your body perish, than for your whole body to be thrown into hell.'"

Ephesians 5:3–5: "But do not let immorality or any impurity or greed even be named among you, as is proper among saints; and there must be no filthiness and silly talk, or coarse jesting, which are not fitting, but rather giving of thanks. For this you know with certainty, that no immoral or impure person or covetous man, who is an idolater, has any inheritance in the kingdom of Christ and God."

"Self-control and modesty do not consist only in purity of the flesh, but also in seemliness and in the modesty of dress and adornment" (Cyprian, A.D. 250).[5]

What are we *allowing* our eyes to take in? What are we watching on television? What are we listening to on the radio? How modest is our dress? Why do we *really* dress the way we do? Nothing I could say in response to your answers to the above questions would enter the same realm of seriousness with which Jesus, Paul, or Cyprian would respond. If Jesus spent the day with you, would you look at, and listen to, the things that you are looking at and listening to now? Would you dress any differently?

Divorce

Matthew 19:9: "'And I say to you, whoever divorces his wife, except for immorality, and marries another woman commits adultery.'"

Luke 16:18: "'Everyone who divorces his wife and marries another commits adultery; and he who marries one who is divorced from a husband commits adultery.'"

"That the scripture counsels marriage and allows no release from the union is expressly contained in the law, you will not put away your wife, except for the cause of fornication. And it regards as fornication the marriage of those separated while the *other is still alive.* Our Lord said, He who takes a woman who has been put away commits adultery" (Clement of Alexandria, A.D. 195).[6]

As the head of a catechetical school, Clement instructed young converts. He is considered by many biblical scholars to be one of the more liberal teachers of the early church. Regarding his obedience to Jesus' teachings concerning divorce, Clement would be considered an ultraconservative in today's church.

The Role of Women in the Church

1 Timothy 2:11, 12: "Let a woman quietly receive instruction with entire submissiveness. But I do not allow a woman to teach or exercise authority over a man, but to remain quiet."

1 Peter 3:1, 2, 5: "In the same way, you wives, be submissive to your own husbands so that even if any of them are disobedient to the Word, they may be won without a word by the behavior of their wives, as they observe your chaste and respectful behavior. For in this way in former times the holy women also, who hoped in God, used to adorn themselves, being submissive to their husbands."

"But the woman of pertness, who has usurped the power to teach, will of course not give birth for herself likewise to a right of baptizing! For how credible would it seem, that he who has not permitted a woman even to learn with over-boldness, should give a female the power of teaching and of baptizing! He says, Let them be silent and consult their husbands at home" (Tertullian, A.D. 200).[7]

I recently had a discussion with a professing Christian concerning the role of women in the church. The last two Scriptures we examined were from 1 Timothy and 1 Peter, referenced above. His core response was, "Paul and Peter are not Jesus." I came back with the wrong response by saying that Jesus sent out twelve, then seventy-two, and none of them were women. And although Jesus had women who took care of His needs and provided an incredible ministry, there is no historical record of Him allowing a woman to teach, preach, baptize, or have any type of authority over men. Then I thought to myself, "Wait just a Jerusalem minute. Paul and Peter are the New Testament; they wrote the *very words of God* as He carried them along in the Holy Spirit (cf. 2 Peter 1:21). If I don't have to obey Paul and Peter, then the Bible is a sham. If Paul and Peter don't hold up the blood-soaked banner of Christ, then I am going to go out tonight and begin my complete descent into the world."

I have never claimed to be a brave man. One area I don't want to be courageous in is deciding which teachings in the New Testament need to be converted to fit twenty-first-century society. There is not enough common sense in the world for me to trust myself to believe that I know what parts of the Bible no longer apply. Which verses, chapters, or books need updating as the world's standards and moral compass change direction from generation to generation? Are we expected to go along with **biblical modifications** to fit the current social and political ideals of society? Have we already met that expectation?

I have lived around hundreds of "Christian" leaders and thousands of "professing Christians" who have subtly and blatantly taken the conversion process into their own hands. I have been a major converter as well. I am desperately striving to stop converting the life and teachings of Jesus. Deep down I want my mind, heart, and life converted to fit exactly what He said and did! The kingdom teachings and life of Christ are incredibly challenging to teach, let alone live.

If ministers decided this Sunday to teach and preach what Jesus and His Word say about baptism, nonviolence, separation from the world, purity, modesty, divorce, and the biblical role of women, then ninety percent of them would lose their jobs by Monday morning. The ones who survived would take a huge pay cut because about half of the congregation would be seeking a new, *more "modern" church home, i.e.* a place that has *converted to their way of thinking.*

For the lay people among us, deciding to teach what Jesus taught is a scary prospect in any generation or society. The one in which we find ourselves engulfed is especially frightening. Ultimately, *choosing not* to teach and live what Jesus taught could be much more frightening when all generations and societies pass and only the heavenly remains. I urge and plead with each of us to search the New Testament to see for ourselves what Jesus, and those He used to write His Word, said and did. If, for some reason, more commentary or examples are needed, go to the early church writers. Go bravely with a heart that is *willing to be converted.*

Let us always remember that Jesus is the same yesterday, today, and forever (Hebrews 13:8). Jesus doesn't change as the political or social climate changes. He is always burning hot! On the contrary, if our convictions and lives are anywhere near lukewarm, they should heat up quickly as we embark on the *bold adventure* of truly listening to and doing exactly what Jesus and His Word tells us to do. Let this verse be a reminder to us: "Then a cloud formed, overshadowing them; and a voice came out of the cloud, 'This is My beloved Son, listen to Him!'" (Mark 9:7).

As we continue on this daily pilgrimage, our lives should never be the same again, nor should the lives of those around us. Discovering, or *rediscovering*, the truth will only hurt us if we don't allow ourselves to be converted. Once He truly converts us, then the truth no longer has to hurt.

18

The Truth Doesn't Have to Hurt

*Men occasionally stumble over the truth, but most of them
pick themselves up and hurry off as if nothing ever happened.*

Winston Churchill

Do we like the truth? The question is not whether we can handle
the truth. But do we like, even love, discovering or hearing the truth?
What about when the *truth exposes* one of our many weaknesses? It
is unlikely that any of us will radically change until we really desire
to hear the truth about who we truly are at a heart level. If we are
striving to be the best we can be for God, ourselves, or somebody
else, we should love hearing and embracing the truth. At what point
does our love of truth begin to diminish?

At what point did we stop telling the truth? At some point social
etiquette pressures us into not being truthful with one another. For me
it can be traced back to receiving a pair of garden work gloves from
my grandma on Christmas. Please don't misunderstand me: a good
pair of work gloves is a vital part of an adult wardrobe, but it just
doesn't usually make it onto the Christmas list of a five-year-old. My
truthful response was to throw them on the floor and proclaim before
all of the family, "What are these?"

I understand that sensitivity is often needed when speaking the truth, but where do we draw the line? How do we make the transition from social lying to a life of teaching and living by the truth? At the end of every question like this awaits "The Truth." Churchill described the *inescapable* nature of truth. "Truth is incontrovertible; malice may attack it and ignorance may deride it; but, in the end, there it is."[1]

History records many things about Winston Churchill; however, failure to speak the truth and also listen to the truth are seldom in the historical record. What is in our **individual historical records** with regard to speaking and listening to the truth? There are two levels of truth. The first one is "The Truth," which is God accompanied closely by His Son, Spirit, and Word. This truth is incontrovertible and in the end will be there waiting for us. In the end if we have been hiding and not seeking, we are going to feel those words we heard so often in childhood, "Ready or not, here I come."

The lower level of truth is that which we seek or get from people, various sources, and life experiences. This is the truth on which I want us to focus now. How do you *respond in your heart* when some truth is pointed out about your character, life, children or *whatever?* How about when you stumble across a truth that is not spoken directly to you but perhaps comes through a book, sermon, or another source? Can we honestly say we love the truth?

We should be able to proclaim a love for the truth loudly and proudly. Don't we spend most of our lives trying to become better people? Why do we so often hurry off as if nothing happened when we discover a truth that could change our lives? Why is it so difficult to accept and act upon truth?

When we resist "The Truth" and truths of life (which we all do), we lack not only humility but courage as well. Churchill also gave the world these historic words of truth:

"Courage is what it takes to stand up and speak;
courage is also what it takes to sit down and listen."[2]

Someone posed the following question to me: "Does it take more courage to speak the truth to people or to listen to the truth from others?" I do not know psychologically which is more difficult. What I do know is that speaking truth or listening to it takes more courage than I sometimes seem to possess.

Perhaps the truth is challenging to speak to others because of the way someone responded to our input in the past. Or maybe the truth is hard to accept because of the way it has sometimes been presented to us. Ultimately, if we really love the truth, it shouldn't matter how it is presented. However, the reality of the human psychological makeup often dictates that it does indeed matter how we present truth.

I believe we all need some true encouragement to gain the courage that is essential to speak and listen to the truth. To battle these two challenges we must return to the source of courage. Do you remember the call to speak the truth in love from Ephesians 4:25? Let's read that verse again in its context.

> If indeed you have heard Him and been taught in Him, just as truth is in Jesus, that, in reference to your former manner of life, you lay aside the old self, which is being corrupted in accordance with the lusts of deceit, and that you be renewed in the spirit of your mind, and put on the new self, which in the likeness of God has been created in righteousness and holiness of the truth. Therefore, laying aside falsehood, speak truth, each one of you, with his neighbor, for we are members of one another. Let no unwholesome word proceed from your mouth, but only such a word as is good for edification according to the need of the moment, that it may give grace to those that hear. And do not grieve the Holy Spirit of God, by whom you were sealed for the day of redemption. Let all bitterness and wrath and anger and clamor and slander be put away

from you, along with all malice. And be kind to one another, tender-hearted, forgiving each other, just as God in Christ also has forgiven you" (Ephesians 4:21–32).

May God have mercy on us all!

Let me give you a practical example of how I have recently received courage from a friend's encouragement. My friend approached me a few weeks ago asking in a loving way if everything was okay. I am not talking about that common superficial conversation that we have all been a part of. It can go something like this: "How are you doing? Good. How are you doing? Good. All right, great!" Are we really saying, consciously or subconsciously, "Let's leave each other alone so we won't be tempted to talk about how we are really doing?" Does this sound familiar? Even in church, that self-proclaimed haven of truth, people rarely get past the "how-ya-doin—good" stage.

This true friend wasn't looking for the "I'm doing fine," conversation. He had just witnessed my impatience with my wife. When we've witnessed impatience or anger or pride in some other form, everything is not "fine." Although this is most likely what the prideful person will tell you if you ask him how he is doing? As difficult as it was to respond humbly, I can now appreciate my friends conviction to speak the truth in love (Ephesians 4:15).

This friend could have come to me and said, "Bob, I saw you get impatient with Rosey. I can't believe you did that in front of everybody; I would never do that to my wife." That would have shut me down like a small, family hardware store when Wal-Mart comes to town. Instead he said, "Bob, I couldn't help but notice that you and Rosey were struggling a bit. Do you need someone to talk to?"

I am so grateful for all the people God has put in my life who are *willing* to speak the truth in love. My encouragement is for you to find people who are willing to give you the courage you will need to live a life of truth. We all need people who are willing to give us the daring we need to live such a life.

Now on to "The Truth". Jesus Christ should be easier to listen to and accept. After all, shouldn't it be easy to trust in something that is absolutely perfect. Without a second thought, I put my two children in their car seats today and proceeded to the highway, where I drove the maximum speed limit of seventy miles per hour. I completely entrusted my precious family to an automobile that is not perfect. In fact, a certain percentage of automobiles will malfunction, causing the deaths of people. Jesus and His Word have never malfunctioned, so it *should be* easy to trust and follow His Word.

Even though Jesus is perfect, I believe very few people truly listen, accept, and obey His specific call. Instead of strictly adhering to and obeying His Word, most of humankind has altered, twisted, converted, or outright ignored portions of it to fit into their way of life. I am not exclusively referring to groups such as the Mormon Church that have created writings or books in addition to the Bible. I am talking to myself and possibly to you and any individual or group that professes to believe in Jesus. Are we obeying and trusting in God's Word even when it goes contrary to societal norms and political pressures?

Consider this principle. God is Truth; we are not. We need to examine our standard of life to make sure we have not created "truths" apart from God's Word. It is the golden rule of truth that God is The Truth and so He makes the rules!

Even more important than our proper response to basic truths of life is our humble response to the ultimate Truth. We need to respond humbly when truth is pointed out to us by others. We need to be humbled as we are allowed to respond to Him. There is only *one acceptable response* to God: listen to Him, embrace Him, and walk with Him!

Isn't it an amazing coincidence that each time I don't listen to and obey exactly what God says, life doesn't seem to work out well. I completely understand and believe in this spiritual consequence, and yet it seems difficult for me to avoid it at times. Can you relate? If so, I encourage you to examine daily your obedience to God's Word.

I have spent the past two years studying the New Testament and writings of the early church leaders. I and the church of which I am a part have always claimed to follow "only the Bible" and to model ourselves after the primitive church. But a question kept surfacing in my conscience that needed to be answered. If I and my church are living by God's Word and claiming to model ourselves after the early church, then why, in so many ways, don't our lives resemble them?

As I pleaded with my Father for an answer to this question, He revealed to me some doctrinal and lifestyle teachings that we weren't applying. God also revealed some things we are doing that we shouldn't be. After digesting a pretty big slice of humble pie, it wasn't real difficult to accept the fact that my life and the lives of those around me in many ways didn't match up to the early church. More importantly, we weren't matching up to the New Testament.

Understanding and accepting God's answer has been the easy part. Acting upon what I claim to believe has proven to be extremely difficult. Some of what God has revealed will hopefully mean changes in my church. Many changes in my family have been and will continue to be required. The most humbling, gut-wrenching part of this essential process is the overwhelming number of radical changes I will *personally need to make*. The promptings of God directed squarely at my heart and life will require *an intimacy with Him that I may never have known before*.

How I long to be utterly unafraid of this level of intimacy. I must realize that this goal is the point of life. This I know—I can and must attain the goal.

19

What Do I Know?

In response to her dad not being able to answer one of her questions: "Dad, you traveled around the world. How can you not know the answer?"

Celise Wilson

What do I know? If you asked my six-year-old daughter, Celise, she would tell you that her dad knows *almost* all of life's answers. If you asked her two-year-old sister, Sonja, what her dad knew, she would try to tell you that daddy knows everything.

What do I really know? Very little! There was a television show that aired when I was a kid called *Hogan's Heroes*. One of the characters, Sergeant Schultz, when asked what he knew about some secret information, would answer, "I know nothing!" Find some old person like me (over forty) and have him imitate Sergeant Schultz. Trust me that he will love to do the imitation. In the meantime, let's say the following together three times:

> I know very little.
> I know very little.
> I know very little.

This is not just my opinion. Listen to what Socrates said toward the end of his life: "The only thing I know for sure is that I know nothing."[1] Vincent Van Gogh left us this inspiring word portrait: "For my part I know nothing with any certainty, but the sight of the stars makes me dream."[2] Maybe it will be easier for brilliant people like these to blow your cover, rather than someone like me who is probably not as smart as you. These quotes remind me of a book entitled *Everything Men Know about Women.* The book has about two hundred pages, and they are all blank.

Coming to terms with how little we really know can actually open a great gate of wisdom. This admission is both challenging and freeing. The feeling is similar to the one when I realized that I will never know as much as I don't know, regardless of how much study is sought.

I recently spent eighteen months reading the *Ante-Nicene Fathers.* This ten volume literary work is over six thousand pages of writings from Christian church leaders dating from approximately A.D. 70 to 325. I then spent six months re-examining the New Testament, trying to **rid myself of any preconceived notions** I had about God and His church. In that two-year period, I learned more about God and how He wants His followers to live than I had learned in my previous forty-one years of life. The other fact that came screaming out toward me was that I will never know as much about God as I don't know, regardless of how much I study His ways.

Martin Luther King Jr. proclaimed these ageless words of wisdom: "Ten thousand fools proclaim themselves into obscurity while one wise man forgets himself into immortality."[3] Jesus Christ was the master of forgetting Himself. He was God in the flesh, walking the earth with more physical, mental, and spiritual power than any other person. He realized that without His Father He would not be what He was created to be. Jesus Christ astonishingly said the following humble and humbling words in John 5:30.

"'I can do nothing on My own initiative. As I hear, I judge; and My judgment is just, because I do not seek My own will, but the will of Him who sent Me.'"

Jesus changed the world forever because He became who He was created to be. When we don't become who *He created us to be,* then we turn out to be of *little eternal consequence.*

The Son of God chose to forget Himself and remember us! It is so hard for me to forget myself. I can be so preoccupied with my own needs and wants. Do you struggle with this as well? Obscurity is not a place that many on earth want or seek to visit, and very rarely will a person choose to live there. Plutarch, a first-century Greek biographer, challenges us with these powerful words: "Learn to be pleased with everything, with wealth so far as it makes us beneficial to others, with poverty for not having much to care for, and with obscurity; for being unenvied."[4]

How does one live in spiritual obscurity? (I am not talking about obscurity where no one knows I am a Christian; everyone I know and every person who is willing to listen to me should clearly and *specifically* know why I am what I am). I need to become more obscure; Jesus needs to become *more obvious* in my life! So how can we become more spiritually obscure? Begin by learning to embrace and fall in love with one very intense, profound verse—John 3:30.

"He [Jesus] must increase, but I must decrease."

My counsel is to strive to live this call. We cannot attain to any higher form of learning than training ourselves to live a life hidden in Christ, as described in Colossians 3:3: "For you have died and your life is hidden with Christ in God."

Ironically, I have never been more inspired to seek knowledge and understanding since discovering how little I know. Knowledge is good but we need to approach it with a different spirit, i.e. a spirit of humility and a spirit of priority. It is vital that we major in what we *need to know* from the *"All-knowing."* Everything else is a lifetime elective to enjoy and maybe keep us from hurting others and ourselves.

Some new form of knowledge or understanding may open a gate unto a new or deeper relationship. Perhaps an elective of learning you are moved to pursue can be used to help someone. Obviously, if we have a desire to truly help people, we should not just give them worldly knowledge, but our hearts' desire should be to guide them to the source of all knowledge. Thomas Kempis gained the following understanding as he sought after this highest form of learning. He educates us all with the following description of God:

> I am He who in one instant do lift up the humble mind to comprehend more reasonings of eternal truth, than if one had studied ten years in the schools. I teach without noise of words, without the confusion of opinions, without the pride of honor, without the scuffling of arguments. I am He who instructs men to despise earthly things, to loath things present, to seek things eternal, to relish things eternal; to flee honors, to endure offenses, to place all hope in Me, out of Me to desire nothing, and above all things ardently to love Me.[5]

As I ardently love Him, all I essentially need to know is how to **receive and maintain** His salvation. Fortunately, my Lord is not only all-knowing, He is also all-loving. God gives me a life test, but in His indescribable love He has made it an open-book entrance and final exam. We don't have to memorize the Bible or even know all of it to receive and maintain His gift of salvation.

Salvation is not a one-time event in my past. Eleven years ago, I responded to my belief that Jesus is who He claims to be by repenting and being baptized. All my sins up to that time were forgiven and I received the gift of God's Holy Spirit. I was born again with the water and the spirit (John 3:5). This initial salvation is wonderful, but it happened eleven years ago. What about the past four-thousand-plus days? What about whatever future days God grants me? The scriptures are very clear about a future aspect of salvation (Matthew 10:22; John 15:5, 6:2; 1 Timothy 4:16; 2 Timothy 2:12; 2 Peter 2:20, 21 ff.). David Bercot, in his book *The Kingdom That Turned The World Upside Down*, writes of John 15:5 and the two stages of salvation.

This passage demonstrates the two aspects of salvation—past and future. Only those who have been born again, who have been saved, can be branches on the vine. That's the past aspect of salvation. Nevertheless, just because we're a branch on Jesus' vine doesn't mean that we are going to stay on the vine. If we don't maintain our obedient love relationship, God will lop us off of the vine. That's why we must also talk of the future aspect of salvation.

A few pages later Mr. Bercot continues as follows: "Asking someone, have you been saved is like asking a person, have you quit stealing from your employer? An honest employee can't answer that question with a simple yes or no, can he? He can only thwart this deceptive question by replying, I have never stolen from my employer, so there's nothing to quit. The salvation question is just as deceptive, although unintentionally so. A simple yes or no will not suffice. Someone who understands the gospel of the kingdom must counter the inherent deceptiveness of the question by responding, yes, I was saved when I was born again. However, my final salvation will not be determined until I have endured to the end.

Before all of us who have been truly born again begin a major panic attack, he goes on to write concerning the issue of salvation, in the context of security.

We kingdom Christians don't live in constant anguish and insecurity. No, we live in joyous anticipation of the promises that Jesus has made. And we know that Jesus' grace will enable us to stay on the vine—so long as we continue to love and obey Him. However, at the same time, we must not become overconfident and presumptuous. Nor should we ever lose our fear of our Lord. Yes, we enjoy true security, but it's conditional security.[6]

The good news is that we need to know very little to enter and maintain a relationship of ongoing salvation with the all-caring Father. The incredible news is that our lives can be exactly what they were designed to be if we obey His Good News.

The Apostle Peter writes in 1 Peter 1:3–5, Blessed be the God and Father of our Lord Jesus Christ, who according to His great mercy has caused us to be born again to a living hope through the resurrection of Jesus Christ from the dead, to obtain an inheritance which is imperishable and undefiled and will not fade away, reserved in heaven for you, who are protected by the power of God through faith for a salvation ready to be revealed in the last time.

The One who promises and delivers this good news will never get old.

20

Everything Gets Old Except God

You may delay time, but time will not.

Benjamin Franklin

Five-star hotels, traveling the world, money, possessions, jobs, hobbies, parents, children, siblings, spouse, and even the family dog—all of these and everything else I have seen and known get old. God doesn't get old! He is enduring and as vibrant as the first days I was introduced to Him. The way I choose to approach and worship Him may *feel* like it is getting stale or old periodically, but God doesn't change during these spiritually down times.

Raise your hand if you would like to spend the next five years staying in four-and-five-star hotels and eating in restaurants with as many stars. Don't panic over the cost: assume that you could live like this completely covered by a company's expense account. Do you think that would get old in five or even fifty five years? I actually experienced the above scenario, and it didn't take five years for it to get old. It actually took about five months, and I am not a person who is easily bored.

Raise your hand again if you would like to quit the above job and travel the world for a few years. Once again, you don't need to worry about anything back home, including money. Do you think that would get old? It did for me. When I first contemplated the opportunity to travel, I couldn't imagine anything more tantalizing than freely exploring the world. Again, I am not prone to boredom, and I have a decent imagination. Traveling got so old that it took me years to even want to leave the city where the trip ended.

For some unexplained reason, I was allowed to experience these incredible circumstances. Maybe it was to teach me that everything gets old except God. I had always questioned existence, purpose, life after death, and indirectly why everything gets old. In looking back, I believe these experiences created more questions than answers. What am I supposed to do with the time allotted to me? *How much time* do I have to figure this question out? How much time do I have, period? When my *time is up,* is that the end of time?

The reality of the "sands of time" has driven much greater minds than mine literally insane for thousands of years. The inability to control time and ultimately death has even led many to the final decision of ending their own lives. Our inability to slow down time can be a scary prospect in the realm of this world, where so much emphasis is placed on youth and vigor. Getting old is a downright frightening reality for anyone without an **eternal retirement plan.**

Stop fighting against the *reality* that everything gets old, including you. Stop trying to turn back the hands of time. Stop fighting with a needless fear of the end of your life. Stop fighting against God's timeless plan and purpose for your life! Stop, stop, stop, stop! God never gets old! If we grow old in this life truly living for God, we will get to live forever with Him in a state of *unutterable bliss!* Stop fretting about aging, and start living for the *ageless One.*

My wife recently asked me, "Do I look like a middle-aged woman in these clothes?" I replied in a very sensitive way that she not only looked like a middle-aged woman, but she actually is middle-aged. I won't tell you her age, but I am forty-three and she married a slightly younger man. What ever happened to aging with grace? I am happy to have made it to the middle-age stage. In fact, I hope I am past middle age, because I want no part of attending my eighty-seventh birthday party. Call me crazy, but I am looking forward to complete and utter bliss in heaven with God. Forget aging with grace; I just want to *die with grace!*

The reality of how little we can actually control is never more magnified than when it is applied to time and death. You and I have fewer tick tocks than when we began this day, this chapter, and this sentence. At the end of our last tick tock awaits death. Death can either be an experience of the coolest of homes in heaven or the hottest of homes in hell. John Donne wittily wrote, "A dead atheist is someone who is all dressed up with no place to go."[1] Actually, there is a place awaiting the atheist and those who didn't live for God and His kingdom, just like there is an eternal home that awaits the one who chose to *die for Christ* before the end of their time on earth.

It is my sober conviction that if one chooses to die for Christ on earth he or she will live with Him for time eternal. If we live and die in and for Him here on earth, He will be waiting to take us home. Thomas Huxley rendered time powerless with the following timeless words: "Time, whose tooth gnaws away at everything else, is powerless against truth."[2] Since reading those words years ago, I have experienced time gnawing away at much that I had once believed, but *The Truth* still stands strong.

Does the reality of time slipping through your hands alarm you? If so, it is time to join forces with the One who created and controls time. He is time, He is eternity. With Him, you and I will never run out of time. I am now able to securely laugh at this next quote. "Time is a great teacher. Unfortunately, it kills all its pupils."[3] Time eventually kills the world's pupils, but it does not harm the *graduates of God!*

"What the caterpillar calls the end of the world,
the master calls a butterfly."[4]

21

The Passionless

Again, the devil took Him to a very high mountain, and showed Him all the kingdoms of the world, and their glory; and he said to Him, "All these things will I give you, if you fall down and worship me." Then Jesus said to him, "Be gone Satan! For it is written, you shall worship the Lord your God, and serve Him only."

Matthew 4:8–10

All of the passions of Jesus were enveloped in his devotion to his Father. I know that it is not realistic for all of our passions to be directed toward God. However, what approximate percentage of them is devoted to God, and what percentage is devoted to the world?

Soon after Jesus left Satan frustrated in the desert, He spoke to a little more receptive crowd.

> "Do not lay up for yourselves treasures upon earth, where moth and rust destroy, and where thieves break in and steal. But lay up for yourselves treasures in heaven, where neither moth nor rust destroys, and where thieves do not break in and steal; for where your treasure is, there will your heart be also" (Matthew 6:19–21).

What are our *true treasures* in this life? What or who possesses our heart? Identify your true heart treasure, and you will answer the question, "With whom do your passions lie?"

What are we *really passionate* about? The answer is revealed in our actions. How do we spend most of our time? I realize many people need to work eight or so hours a day, but what is your passion at work? Are you there to make money to pay off your debts? Are you there to build your resume' or advance a career? Or is your *main motivation* to build relationships, with the goal of winning people to Christ? Jesus gives us a convicting command in Matthew 6:31–33:

> "Do not be anxious then, saying, what shall we eat? Or what shall we drink? Or with what shall we clothe ourselves? For all these things the Gentiles eagerly seek; for your heavenly Father knows that you need all these things. But seek first His kingdom and His righteousness; and all these things shall be added to you."

Not only do we need to analyze how we spend our time, but a deeper analysis of what *really excites* us may be a better test of where our passions lie. What do we really get excited about? Do we get *more excited* about working to build God's house or our own? Do we get more excited sharing about what our kids have done or what Jesus has done? Is it a toss-up between our excitement level worshiping God on Sunday morning or rooting for our favorite team later that afternoon? Do you find the time to clean up the house, car, and yard, but there just doesn't seem to be enough hours in your day to clean up the spiritual messes? Are our passions reserved for the world *or* for God and His kingdom?

The questions above and many others you and I could ask ourselves prompted me to ask another question: "Would the world be better off with less passion?" Would we be better off if we were *passionless for the world?* Okay, if I would just answer "no" to that question, many of you would agree and we could move on to the next chapter. Let us take some time together and further examine the concept of passion and living passionless for the world.

The word *passionless* means "*unbiased* or *impartial; detached.*" This doesn't sound like a very exciting journey. Why did Jesus, the apostles, and the people that made up the early church choose to be passionless when it came to matters that the world cared about? This question is reason enough for me to examine the issue in more detail.

Jesus didn't *desire* the kingdoms of the world. He didn't aspire to be a king in a worldly sense. He said His followers would not be of the world, just as He was not of the world. He told Pilate that if His kingdom was of this world, His followers would fight to protect Him.

The apostles didn't seem concerned about the struggle of their Jewish kinsmen for worldly independence. They also didn't seem overly concerned about their safety, livelihood, or life for that matter. There is no record of them or anyone who followed after them having any passion for things outside of Christ and His kingdom. They chose a passionless detachment from things of the world.

The following are only a few of the Scriptures that inspired the early church to live passionless toward the world:

Luke 9:24: "'For whoever wishes to save his life shall lose it, but whoever loses his life for My sake, he is the one who will save it.'"

1 Corinthians 2:2: "For I determined to know nothing among you except Jesus Christ, and Him crucified."

Colossians 3:5: "Therefore consider the members of your earthly body as dead to immorality, impurity, passion, evil desire, and greed which amount to idolatry."

Philippians 1:21: "For to me, to live is Christ, and to die is gain."

There are hundreds of other passages and examples that paint a passionless picture; many of these life paintings were finished in blood.

There are also hundreds of writings from the early church which paint a duplicate portrait. A second-century disciple gave his personal convictions as a follower of Christ. This could have been written by the overwhelming majority of disciples throughout the first three centuries.

> I do not wish to be a king. I am not anxious to be rich. I decline military command. I detest fornication. I am not impelled by an insatiable love of gain to go to sea. I do not contend for awards. I am free from the mad thirst of fame. I despise death. I am superior to every kind of disease. Grief does not consume my soul. If I am a slave, I endure servitude. If I am free, I do not boast about my good birth. Die to the world, repudiating the madness that is in it! Live to God!"[1]

Later in the second-century, an elder named Clement of Alexandria gave the following instruction to Christians, many of whom were being tortured and killed:

> How preposterous and absurd it is, that while we ask that the will of God should be done, yet when God calls and summons us from this world, we do not at once obey the command of His will. Do we wish to be honored with heavenly rewards by Him to whom we come unwillingly? Why, then, do we pray and ask that the kingdom of heaven may come, if the captivity of earth delights us?[2]

Are we captivated by the many delights of the world? Where does our true passion *live?* Is the lion's share of our passion dispersed within the world *or* concentrated on God's kingdom and bringing Him glory?

The *battle* for distribution of passion is waged everyday for our minds and hearts. Are we willing to fight to be more passionless toward the world? If we are willing, I believe God will teach us some of the secrets that He whispered to His earliest victors! Some nineteen hundred years after the resurrection of Jesus, Someone whispered a secret to Thomas Kempis:

> "Oh if Jesus crucified would come into our hearts how quickly and fully should we be taught."[3]

Is the concept of living passionless with regard to things in the world still hard to grasp with your mind and heart? I know it is for me, even after recognizing it in the teachings and life of Jesus, the apostles, and hundreds of thousands of ordinary men and women of the early church. Like most everything else that our secular society teaches and stands for, living passionless toward the things of the world is contrary to secular teachings.

For those not seeking a surrendered and separate life in Christ, living passionless must seem like an insane premise. Why would a person who doesn't believe in life after death not choose a life devoted to worldly pleasure? The premise of passionless living is probably getting those particular readers' blood boiling. I would ask that you not become overly passionate and jump to conclusions. Let me share my personal story of seeking worldly passions before you make any additional life decisions based on emotion.

I have pursued just about every passion the world has used to lure mankind. I have been engrossed at some point in life with hobbies, sports, entertainment, dating, marriage, alcohol, drugs, fun, popularity, political solutions, learning, and of course, the thread that tied it all together—me! As I was living only for this lifetime, with all my passion directed toward attaining happiness now, I lived in almost constant insecurity, discontentment, hopelessness, fear, and/or loneliness.

Choosing to be passionless for worldly desires doesn't leave much room for insecurity, discontentment, or any other negative state of being. When our zeal is focused on God, it is difficult to be hurt by the entrapments of the world. Kempis concisely stated, "It is no hard matter to despise human comfort when we have divine."[4] Jesus, the apostles, and their followers chose, and **we ultimately choose**, what we will be passionate about. It is precisely those choices that will determine *our mark on history, our impact on today,* and most likely, *our eternal address.*

I was recently asked if passion was a good or bad emotion. I answered, "Yes." Passion is an absolute godsend if and when it is sent toward God. On the opposite side, passion can be a very detrimental emotion if it is selfishly directed toward worldly pursuits. The emotion is not bad in and of itself. It is not what kind or how much passion but the direction it is focused that matters. Is our passion for the world or for God? I believe it is dangerous at the very least to try to have both. If we are not careful to keep our passions in the right priority, one of them may guide us away from the ultimate goal. Getting ourselves and others to heaven should be the goal that is in *some way connected to all of our passion.*

It may be possible to make it to heaven having zealousness for both God and some good things of the world. It would be biblically implausible to make it Home if our greater zeal was not reserved for God. As a sober reminder to us all, Jesus and the massive throngs of early followers were zealous for one predominate thing—God!

Mel Gibson received much criticism, mainly from non-Christians, for his movie *The Passion* (the death of Christ for the world). The concept of the passionless (the death of man to the world) will probably receive much criticism from non-Christians and Christians alike. I ask that you take the time to examine the passionless calling in an eternal context. It is worth the investment of time because one's passion often leads to action. These actions have an incredible impact on the events of our lives, as well as the lives of so many around us. Passion can be very contagious!

If our passion is immersed in and for the world, those we love and need to love will be more influenced toward the same misdirected life. We have the privilege to help guide people's passions toward God. The way we decide to direct our passions will and is leaving a mark on those whom God has given us to love. We can all make changes now before some of these marks leave *lifelong scars.*

The decision Jesus made to surrender Himself to the cross clarified His passion. Thomas Kempis tried to bring clarity and simplicity to life as he wrestled in word with the cross.

> In the cross is salvation, in the cross is life, in the cross is protection against our enemies, in the cross is infusion of heavenly sweetness, in the cross is strength of mind, in the cross is joy of spirit, in the cross the height of virtue, in the cross the perfection of holiness. There is no salvation of soul, or hope of everlasting life, but in the cross. Behold in the cross all consists, and in our dying thereon all lies! For there is no other way unto life, and unto true inward peace, but the way of the cross and of daily mortification. Walk where you will, seek whatever you will, you shall not find a higher way above, or a safer way below, than the way of the cross.[5]

Is our passion *the passion of Christ?* This godly passion will clarify, and therefore simplify, our priorities and life!

22

Simplicity is Flexible

Simplicity is flexible. It endures well. Without so many things around we have more time.

Warren Least Heat Moon

Here is a common definition of *simplicity:* "The property, condition or quality of being simple or uncluttered." Let's all sigh together: those were the days. Or maybe we haven't lived many days of simplicity, but it sure sounds great! If simplicity seems out of your circumstantial grasp, at the bare minimum, strive to simplify. *Simplify* simply means to reduce in complexity or extent; to reduce to fundamental parts." We all *can and should* simplify.

Just before my thirtieth birthday, I decided to simplify my life. I quit what my family defined as the "dream job" and sold almost all my possessions that had accumulated near me. I went from approximately five thousand to fifty pounds of stuff. The breakdown was twenty-two pounds of clothes and supplies to travel the world and about twenty-eight pounds of books. I remember so vividly the feeling of flexibility as the fifty pounds lay before me in clear sight. It was all paid for and none of the stuff needed insurance. I wasn't stressed about protecting my belongings or having to work one or even two jobs to pay for them. Now that was a good day!

Please don't misunderstand me, I do not want to receive any letters beginning with, "Thanks, Bob, for the inspiration to sell my stuff, leave my wife and kids, and travel around the world." I was single at the time, and besides, simplicity doesn't have to be carried around in a backpack. If we cannot master a life of simplicity with a job, spouse, kids and stuff, then we will not be able to live a simple life even if our responsibilities and possessions were gone. Simplicity is a condition of the heart!

If someone took the time to trace his family's genealogy, he would find a few great-grandparents who could live *anywhere* in contentment. However, he would find more ancestors on the family tree that were worldly, insecure, never quite satisfied, and discontented. These particular relatives probably would be found living somewhere surrounded by a lot of stuff.

What happened was that the stuff they had was getting older, duller, and/or smaller than their neighbors' stuff. The eyes of their hearts were not as clear as the grandparents of contentment. Grandpa Contentment was satisfied with whatever amount of goods God had allowed him to use. He realized that no amount of possessions could ever make him feel *truly secure.* Old Grandpa C. understood that the simple life was a matter of heart. He was convinced that what really matters is faith, family, and friends. What really matters to us?

Grandpa C. had more than fifty pounds of stuff, and yet he most likely lived a life of more simplicity and contentment than I was living after I made the "outward decision" to sell my excess baggage. Truly living a life of simplicity and contentment is mostly about what is on the inside. As we are striving to get our hearts in tune with Grandpa Contentment, we can all make *inward decisions to simplify.*

Even though it is vital to understand that simplicity and contentment flow from the inside, it is also important to address the outward decisions to simplify. Let me speak about technology for a moment. Technology can be very costly in money, time, and even purity. Technological advances are not inherently bad. They have advanced our society and most of the world in some great ways. But have they made people's lives simpler or more satisfied?

Does the latest, greatest, biggest and fastest technology really make us happier deep down? My observation of the world is that **people with less technology are happier.** When backpacking in Africa, I witnessed kids kicking a rusty tin can around for hours, seemingly content with their mode of entertainment. In America, kids are bored silly with stacks of video games and hundreds of channels of television. They are not only bored, but they are typically ungrateful unless they have _____. I also witnessed African women working nonstop from sun up to beyond sundown, laughing and singing. How could they have been happy? They didn't even have a microwave, or the electricity to run it for that matter.

Stop for a moment: I am not saying that everyone in Africa is happy and content because they have few, if any, technological toys. I am not suggesting we sell all of our possessions and move to a monastery, but can't we all *strive for less?* Simplicity is not going to solve all of our issues of discontentment; however, doesn't it seem reasonable that working toward a simplified heart and life could bring a *deeper* yearning for and attainment of spiritual contentment?

Most of us have heard the definition of *insanity* as doing the same thing over and over, expecting a different result. There is definitely some truth in that wisdom. Here is how I define insanity: "The chaos created when we define the unnecessary as necessary." What is truly necessary? Are at least some of the things we do over and over in life, regardless of the result, unnecessary?

A simple, yet invaluable, question to pose to ourselves throughout each day is, *"Is this necessary?"* Is this thought necessary? Is this activity necessary? Is this monthly expenditure necessary? Is this third or maybe second vehicle necessary? Is a new model car necessary when the old one is running fine? Is this size or type of house necessary? Without all of the unnecessary monthly expenditures, would working overtime or a part-time job be necessary? Would our spouses need to financially support the family if we were content with the older car, the simpler house, and/or less stuff? How much have we sacrificed for the *self-defined* necessities named above?

Would you be buying it, doing it, or living it if you didn't care what anyone else thought? How about the following question: do the people whose approval we are concerned about getting even notice that we are running around trying to please, impress, or be more like them? I say we should simplify our lives and not get caught up in the *self-induced pressure* created by a materialistic society. I say we should take what is necessary and depend on God for our security and contentment.

On another good day, I realized that I *don't need* most of what I want. Deep down, I *don't even want* a lot of the things I feel like I want. In eighth grade a teacher read an excerpt from a book that basically said, "If half of a person's wishes came true they would be twice as worse off." I am not sure why this is one of the few things I retained from sixteen years of public education. Maybe, it is so that we could analyze the supposition in light of a simple life. I am not statistically sure about the above quote, but instead of thinking in terms of more in life, *imagine simplicity.*

Thomas Kempis described simplicity and purity in the following manner:

> By two wings a man is lifted up from things earthly; namely, by simplicity and purity. Simplicity ought to be in our intention; purity in our affection. Simplicity tends toward God; purity apprehends and tastes Him. No good action will hinder you, if you be inwardly free from inordinate affection. If you intend and seek nothing else but the will of God and the good of your neighbor, you shall thoroughly enjoy inward liberty.[1]

Have we opened *the gift* of inward liberty? Can we at least imagine inward liberty? Imagine how we could reduce the stress in our lives by simplifying our thoughts and actions. Envision being content with just the amount of food, clothing, and shelter we have today or even had at our poorest time? Think of the time and resources that could be freed up if we were content with living closer to the way that over half of the world's population lives with regard to the necessities of life?

Imagine the gratitude that would flow from our hearts as we enjoyed our comparable luxury? Picture using the time and money created from a heart of simplicity for more noble endeavors. Think of the trickle-down effect that a simpler life and contented heart would have on family and friends. *Imagine the impact* on our families and society if one income was once again sufficient?

As a dear friend of mine is fond of saying, "Get off your imagination and go!" Stop imagining and start simplifying your thoughts, actions, and life today. Add a fourth necessity to your list of needs: food, shelter, clothing, and simplicity. Make a list of what you believe you need and another list of what you want. Be honest in identifying what you consider needs and wants. For many of us, our *perceived needs* will be greater than what we define as a want.

How long is your perceived-needs list? You may be suffering from a severe case of *"the wants."*

23

You've Got the Wants

Want is a growing giant whom the coat of have was never large enough to cover.

Ralph Waldo Emerson

The title of this chapter is dedicated to my dad. He often used to tell me and my friends that we had "the wants." "Dad can I have _____?" He would reply, "Sounds like you've got the wants, son." Let me take a moment to more clearly distinguish wants from needs.

Wants are those things that we desire greatly or for which we wish. Needs are those things that are necessary for survival.

My wife and I have frequently examined and re-examined the distinction between wants and needs in our ten years of marriage. In fact, this distinction between needs and wants was pointed out by Jim, the minister who married us. During our first marriage counseling session I asked Jim what we needed to get married. He said, "All you need to get married is a preacher, a witness, and a man and woman. I will be the preacher, my wife can be the witness, and you and Rosey are the man and woman. *You already have all that you need* to get married; everything else is icing on the cake." My wife wanted some things beyond the basic cake, and I wanted to have enough money for our honeymoon. The lesson of needs versus wants helped us end up somewhere between the bare essentials and a wedding well *within our means.*

We needed very little to be married, and we need almost as little to function in life. Again, we need shelter, food, clothing, and very little of any of these to survive. We should also require very little of these necessities to be content. How much do you require to be content? Thousands of years ago Socrates spoke about inward wealth: "Contentment is natural wealth, luxury is artificial poverty."[1] The apostle Paul wrote the following rich words in 1 Timothy 6:6–11.

> But godliness actually is a means of great gain, when accompanied by contentment. For we have brought nothing into the world, so we cannot take anything out of it either. And if we have food and covering, with these we shall be content. But those who want to get rich fall into temptation and a snare and many foolish and harmful desires which plunge men into ruin and destruction. For the love of money is a root of all sorts of evil, and some by longing for it have wandered away from the faith, and pierced themselves with many a pang. But flee from these things, you man of God; and pursue righteousness, godliness, faith, love, perseverance and gentleness.

Following the thought of Socrates and the spirit of Paul, I believe that most of the time we don't actually need what we want. I also believe that people usually aren't **content with just having the true necessities of life.** Do you have the wants? We all do to some degree. Ben Franklin answered the question for everyone in these simple, yet profound words: "Our necessities never equal our wants."

Having the wants is part of the human makeup. I am not advocating that having things outside the basic necessities is bad; I simply want to help us examine what are truly wants and what are our actual needs. What may seem like a small squabble over words makes a huge difference in our level of contentment in life. For example, we may believe we need a bigger or different style of house, perhaps to store all the things we needed to buy, but rarely used. Obviously, we don't need a bigger house. Shelter is indeed a need; big shelter is a want. Redecorating or refurnishing our shelter is not a need.

How we define our true needs weighs heavy on the contentment scale. If we believe we *need* a bigger house and we do not get it, contentment will have a hard time finding a spot in our hearts. However, if we *want* a bigger house and do not get it, then contentment has a chance to find a place in our hearts. Contentment is realizing and accepting that I didn't get what I wanted, but the house I have *been given* is all I really need. Do you see and *believe* the difference?

What about the other two needs: clothing and food? Did our clothes go out of style last season? Don't feel bad because my wardrobe abruptly ended in the mid-eighties. I am convinced that if my wife has enough patience, my clothes will be hip again someday. Anyway, we do not need the latest fashions. We may want to stay on the cutting edge of style, but all we actually need is clothing to cover our bodies, in a modest fashion. The third need is food. We definitely need to eat, but we don't need to eat out more or go to restaurants at all for that matter.

We want many things throughout our lives and that is okay. I am not advocating a weakness of character if we buy a new shirt, paint our house, or go out to eat. The point is that you and I have our needs met a thousand times over. The question we should be reminding ourselves with is, do we have our needs met? **Yes!** Are we grateful for all the *wants we get to have?* If not, go back over what you really need. After that take an inventory of what you actually have. By that time, you should be getting convicted and a lot more grateful.

We have all of our needs covered. If you reside in America, you can also get most of the things you want; assuming your case of the wants is not too severe. An important question to ask is what will this investment truly cost me? Before investing, it would be wise to sit down and count the monetary and *spiritual costs.* I will give two examples that may or may not apply to your life situation. These can help you in examining the cost of investing in whatever wants that you are thinking of pursuing.

Let's start with the housing issue since that is one of the biggest monetary and time investments people make in their lives. Asking questions is the best way to *count the cost.* How big of a house does my family *really need?* How much per month can we *actually afford?* How much more will the utilities be for the added space? How much time are the extra square feet of house and yard going to require to clean and manage? Where is this time going to come from? Will I have to work overtime or get a second job to make the additional payments? Is my spouse going to have to work to pay for the extra space we really don't need? When my wife and I are working the extra hours, *who* is going to be raising our kids?

Do we still want the newer, bigger house? How badly do we feel we need it after more careful consideration? We still may get the house, but at the very least we know the sacrifices it entails. A couple of years ago, our family of four moved from a 1550 square-foot home into an 1800 square-footer. Do you know why? You guessed it: we needed the space. We didn't really need the extra storage, although we may in time. In reality, we do not really need more storage or space. Do you know how I can say with confidence that we don't need 1800 square feet of house for our family of four? Because in over half of the world thirty to forty people live in 1550 square feet of shelter and are grateful to have covering from the elements. We don't need a bigger, newer, or *any other adjective* placed before our shelter.

Food, shelter, and clothing—no adjectives needed! Again, get the bigger house if we want, but count the cost in money, time, and spiritual well-being of our families *before* making the sacrifice.

The other example is fresh on my mind because telemarketers call us weekly to sell us on the need for satellite television. I personally don't have to count any cost to answer no to satellite, digital, cable or any other type of smarter idiot box. But for demonstration sake let's count together.

How much does a personal satellite cost? Let's count the monetary expense first. One of the telemarketers said it was only $30 per month and that it would come out to only $1 per day. I have never bought anything over the phone, but I am learning a lot about math and budgeting during my weekly conversations. The next question she asked was, "Mr. Wilson, do you drink coffee?" I said "no" just to throw her off, and then she let me know that if I did, I could pay for my satellite by simply cutting out one cup a day. I know a lot of couples who are in massive debt after cutting out many cups of coffee. Some of the people I know actually drink more coffee now, drinking some of it during the second job they have acquired to pay for the dollar-a-day investments!

In my opinion, **money is the least of the costs** related to having satellite television. I had an incredibly hard time not growing addicted to and eventually giving up four television channels. How much time would I be spending watching the hundreds of channels to which a satellite would give me access? How much of this time could have been spent with family? Let me answer the thought many of you just had: do you really believe that watching television with your family builds relationships? What about the spiritual or even worldly opportunities we could have experienced while we were entranced in front of our new investment? *Losses* like failing to think about and living for God, missing family time, or not building friendships are *very hard to recover!*

How much will being able to view all the world has to offer decrease our moral convictions and basic purity? That we now measure morality in *how much* our purity is affected instead of *if* our purity is affected should alone be a cost too great to assume. How does watching beautiful people with bigger and better stuff affect our marriages and overall level of contentment?

Can I sell you a satellite system today? It only costs one cup of coffee per day, right? Wrong! It will cost us time, deeper family relationships, spiritual opportunities, purity, and/or contentment. Do we still want it? How badly do we feel we need it after a deeper counting of the cost? Is it *really worth it?* In my opinion, *absolutely not.*

Let us all make the investment to examine what we really need, make sure we can spiritually afford what we want, and *learn to be content* with what we have been given!

24

American Idols

Security outside of complete surrender to Christ is simply another example of a false god.

Bob Wilson

From the beginning of religious history, idolatry has been an issue for mankind. Even in biblical times, God consistently warned against the worship of idols. Most of the human race has ignored the warning calls. In Exodus 20: 3–5a God commands, "You shall have no other gods before Me. You shall not make for yourself an idol, or any likeness of what is in heaven above or on the earth beneath or in the water under the earth. You shall not worship them or serve them; for I, the Lord your God, am a jealous God."

Many would probably look at the book of Exodus as an outdated historical writing. No one worships idols anymore, do they? An *idol* can be defined as any false god, i.e. something adored, often blindly and excessively, in the place of the true God. *The act of idolatry* is blind or excessive devotion to something. Welcome to America. The mass majority of Americans suffer from idolatry, and many of our countrymen want to actually become an *American idol.*

To what are you excessively devoted? What do you truly adore? If the answer to these two questions is not God and His kingdom, then **we are committing idolatry.** Here is a common, abbreviated list of our possible idols:

> careers, money, entertainment, sports, possessions, hobbies, education, kid's activities, relationships, and ourselves.

In the past I have idolized all ten listed above; in the present I still wrestle with a few from time to time. Unfortunately, it *only takes one* idol to step on God's big toes.

In the pages of this book, we have examined separation from the world from many different angles. Idolatry is where the so-called "rubber meets the road." We can technically love things in the world, possibly even be passionate about them. When any love or passion attains a place in the same spiritual universe with God, then we have a problem. More importantly, God has a problem!

In the twentieth century, A.W. Tozer wrote more specifically about the slanderous nature of idolatry: "Idolatry is of all sins the most hateful to God because it is in essence a defamation of the divine character. It holds a low opinion of God, and when it advertises that opinion, it is guilty of circulating an evil rumor about the majesty in the heavens. Thus it slanders the deity. No wonder God hates it."[1] Our present society has carried on this hated tradition of idolatry with *pride and abundance.*

The purpose of this book is not to talk about the phenomenon of American Idol or to try and change our culture. Part of the book's design is to question what is really important and of true lasting value to us. What, if anything, do we idolize? Are we devoted to *anything* more than to God? How can we answer questions that try to define our level of idolatry? We need one more question to begin to form the answer. What do we get excited about in life? I raise this question once again because it is vital that we examine this issue. Take a moment to reflect on the things in life that excite you most. I would imagine that we get excited about many of the same things. The problematic element of idolatry is that many times we end up idolizing things that are good.

For example, I struggle with committing idolatry with my kids. I am inwardly frightened at the intense wellsprings of emotion I feel for my Celise and Sonja. I am devoted to taking care of them and our relationship. I drive friends crazy with stories relating to the amazing coincidence that I would happen to have the two most beautiful, intelligent girls on the planet. I long to talk with them. I love listening to them. I cherish holding and being held by them.

It would be hard for any sane person to argue against the goodness of striving to be a loving father. Being a loving father is admirable and is even an expectation of God. But loving to be a father more than loving The Father is where *admirable devotion ends.*

There are many other examples of idolatry that we could explore together, like other relationships, possessions, pursuing individual achievement, or wealth. No devotion should get more personal than that which we have for our children. Again, commitment to our children is commendable. Even striving to do things well in life is to be applauded. I may go as far as accepting the notion that the desire to attain possessions is not inherently wrong. The question is where do hard work and love and devotion and striving to be the best we can be cross into the **sin of idolatry?** It is a challenging question to define, but it is well worth our time to invest in the challenge. What could be a better way to invest our time than making sure we aren't worshiping anything before or above God?

Let's try to further define the question with additional questions. How easily could we give up our idols? (Obviously, I am not talking about our children). If your idol is a possession, how upset do you get if it is damaged? Do we allow the idol to get in the way of our needed passion to serve God and people? How much time do we invest pursuing and taking care of our idols?

I believe we have been conditioned to be consumers of and *consumed with idolatry.* Centuries ago consumption was a disease that would kill people physically. Today, I am convinced that the desire of material consumption is killing millions spiritually. Oftentimes, we believe that the consumption of something, instead of being the cause of the spiritual disease, will actually cure what is ailing us. *With what are we consumed?* Maybe the consumptive idol is not physical. It could be recognition, honors, to be loved, a secure future, comfort, position, revenge, or seeking forgiveness.

The physical idols are easier to detect, but no less a burden to shed. We can easily be consumed with the appearance of our homes, yards, vehicles, or ourselves. Many are **disproportionately devoted** to education, careers, family activities, entertainment, or sports. I once heard from the pulpit, of all places, that we should be *as passionate* about God as we are about our sports teams. *What did he say?!* It is sad that no one in the audience that morning blurted out, "What did he say?!!"

I believe each of us needs to take a serious, honest look at what we idolize and/or what consumes us. What we discover may *seem innocent and harmless* at first glance, but left unchanged the consumption could end up spiritually killing us and some of those we are closest to. If the consumption is idolized, we need to put it down like a horse with a bad broken leg. Put it out of it's misery before it continues to cause you and your loved ones needless pain.

Whatever idol identified, whether it be a person, place or thing, decide today to stop the idolization. A church leader in the year A.D. 200 pleaded with the people of his day with these solemn words:

> The principal crime of the human race, the highest guilt charged upon the world, the whole procuring cause of judgment, is idolatry. For, although each single fault retains its own proper feature, although it is destined to judgment under its own proper name also, yet it is marked off under the general account of idolatry.[2]

Every religious reader would quickly answer "no" to the following question: "Do you love _____ more than you love God?" Unfortunately, the question is ultimately *answered not with our mouths, but with our lives.* It is our lives that judge us now and that will be the eternal rod of judgment. The question is not do we love created things. The question is do our lives demonstrate that _____ is even on the same radar screen of love that we have for the creator?

Are our innermost dreams *completely fulfilled through Christ* or have they carried us outside of contentment in Him? *True contentment* can be found only in Jesus Christ. If you are seeking fulfillment *outside of the way, the truth, and the life,* may all your dreams **not** come true!

Epilogue

You can not escape the responsibility of tomorrow by evading it today.

Abraham Lincoln

At the Day of Judgment, we will not be asked what we have read but rather what we have done. What will you do with this book? I make no claims to have written complete or absolute truth. (That has already been done, and a sequel is not needed or even possible.) I have simply tried to point our energies toward the eternal by sharing my heartfelt thoughts and convictions. I have also shared ideas from other people throughout the ages who have wrestled for contentment on this crazy, confusing planet. Most importantly, I have endeavored to present *Jesus Christ unadulterated.*

I offer you whatever truths that I and those who have inspired me have ventured across. I also passionately invite you to **seek and follow** after Christ, The Lord! He is the ultimate truth to be acted upon! Many years ago, I either read or wrote this urgent invitation:

"The offer has been made; the right moment to accept it is the moment it is understood; later might be too late."

We understand enough to at least get started on our one-way, eternal pilgrimage.

If there are things we don't understand from this book or The Book, God will make the answers clear if we are truly seeking. May the words of the Apostle Paul in Philippians 3:10–17 be an encouragement to us:

> I want to know Christ and the power of his resurrection and the fellowship of sharing in his sufferings, becoming like him in his death, and so, somehow, to attain to the resurrection from the dead. Not that I have already obtained all this, or have already been made perfect, but I press on to take hold of that for which Christ Jesus took hold of me. Brothers, I do not consider myself yet to have taken hold of it. But one thing I do: forgetting what is behind and straining toward what is ahead, I press on toward the goal to win the prize for which God has called me heavenward in Christ Jesus. All of us who are mature should take such a view of things. And if on some point you think differently, that too God will make clear to you. Only let us live up to what we have already attained. Join with others in following my example, brothers, and take note of those who live according to the pattern we gave you (NIV).

We can end where we began; you and I are responsible. It is our responsibility to act on the truths as The Truth reveals them to us. We need to come to terms with the state of *discontentment the world creates and is in.* Once we recognize and identify where and how the world has been pulling us from God, we must act swiftly to die to the dreams of the world and live passionately for the dreams He has commanded for our lives.

If you are like me, embarking on the purpose and mission we were created for is both exciting and scary. Traveling away from the expansive roads filled with the idols of the world and onto the way of Christ will be *lonely some of the time and narrow all of the time.* If you at any time find yourself traveling on a crowded road, it is likely that you have taken a wrong turn onto a "Converted-Jesus Trail."

Don't panic, because He is eager to guide you back onto the narrow way that has been cleared for His devoted followers.

Truly following the Word and life of Jesus will seem scary and lonesome at times. As we feel scared or lonely, let's remember to talk to the One who truly cares. The heavenly Father is eager to listen to His obedient children. He is willing to allow us to wear His crown of contentment. This crown is found only in His Son Jesus! What about all of the pursuits, ambitions, and attainments in the world? In the end, they are only a dream.

I will begin to bid you farewell with these words of Henry David Thoreau: "I went to the woods because I wished to live deliberately, to confront only the essential facts of life, and see if I could not learn what it had to teach, and not, when I came to die, discover that I had not lived."[1] Mr. Thoreau went to live in the woods to confront what he defined as facts of life. I believe we must live in The Word and allow Christ to define the truths of life. The fact of life is that **someday He is going to confront all of us!**

My version of Thoreau's quote would read as follows: I went to The Word because I wished to live securely, to confront only the essential truths of *The Life*, and see if I could obey what He had to command, and not, when I came to die, discover that I would not live eternally.

The End…A New Beginning?

Personal invitation to the reader

I sincerely desire to receive your feedback and suggestions. Not only regarding how I could have written a better book, but also how I can be a better human being. I will respond to your comments and questions. I pray the Scriptures, convictions, and challenges contained within this book move you in some small or great way to be different, and to make a difference.

Please contact me at cel.ise@verizon.net

Selected Bibliography

Primary Sources

Ante-Nicene Fathers. Edited by Alexander Roberts, D.D. & James Donaldson, LL.D. Peabody, MA: Hendrickson Publishers, Inc., 1994.

Bercot, David W. *A Dictionary of Early Christian Beliefs.* Peabody, MA: Hendrickson Publishers, Inc., 1998.

_____, *The Kingdom That Turned The World Upside Down.* Tyler, TX: Scroll Publishing Company, 2003.

Churchill, Winston. *Churchill Speaks: Winston S. Churchill in Peace and War: Collected Speeches, 1897–1963.* Atheneum, 1981.

Geissler, Rex. *Born of Water.* Great Commission Illustrated, 1996.

Kempis, Thomas A. *of the Imitation of Christ.* New Kensington, PA: Whitaker House, 1981. Page numbers 59, 69, 78, 86, and 175. "Used by permission of Whitaker House (www.whitakerhouse.com)."

Lamsa's, George M. *Holy Bible from the Ancient Eastern Text.* San Fran Cisco: Harper & Row Publishers, 1933.

Lewis, C.S. *Mere Christianity.* New York: Harper Collins publishers, 2001.

Tolstoy, Leo. *The Kingdom of God Is Within You.* University of Nebraska Press, 1985.

Tozer, A.W. *This World: Playground or Battleground?* Christian Publications.com, 1988. Reprinted from This World: Playground or Battleground? By A.W. Tozer, copyright 1989 by Zur, Ltd. Used by permission of WingSpread Publishers, a division of Zur, Ltd., 800.233.4443.

Secondary Sources

Bercot, David W. *Common Sense: A New Approach to Understanding Scripture.* Tyler, TX: Scroll Publishing Company, 1992.

Curtis, Ben; Eldredge, John. *The Sacred Romance.* Nashville, TN: Thomas Nelson, Inc., 1997.

Franklin, Benjamin. *The Autobiography of Benjamin Franklin.* New York: R.F. Collier & Son Company, 1909.

Jacoby, Douglas. *The Spirit.* Woburn, MA: Discipleship Publications, Inc., 1998.

Kriete, Henry. *Worship The King.* Woburn, MA: Discipleship Publications, Inc., 2000.

McDowell, Josh. *Evidence That Demands a Verdict, Volume 1: Historical Evidences for The Christian Faith.* Nelson Reference, 1992.

Swindoll, Charles. *Intimacy With The Almighty.* Thomas Nelson Jack Countryman, 2000.

Thoreau, Henry David. *Walden.* New York: Houghton Mifflin Company, 1949.

Van Gogh, Vincent. *Dear Theo.* New York: Penguin Group, 1995.

Wenger, John Christian. *Even Unto Death.* John Knox Press, 1961.

Notes

Introductory Greeting:

1. Higgison, Thomas Wentworth. *The Writings of Thomas Wentworth Higgison.* Houghton Mifflin Company, 1900.

Chapter 1: It's My Fault

1. Sanford, Charles B. *The Religious Life of Thomas Jefferson.* Charlottesville, VA: The University Press of Virginia, 1984.

2. Kempis, Thomas A. *of the Imitation of Christ.* New Kensington, PA: Whitaker House, 1981.

Chapter 4: Lost Somewhere in the World

1. Van Gogh, Vincent. *The Letters of Vincent Van Gogh.* London: The Penguin Group, 1997.

2. Tertullian. *Ante-Nicene Fathers* (Volume 3, page 46). Peabody, MA: Hendrickson Publishers, Inc., 1994.

3. Pascal, Blaise. *The Provincial Letters.* Nuvision Publications, LLC., 2004.

4. Saint Augustine. *The Catholic Encyclopedia* (Volume 1). Robert Appleton Company, 1907.

Chapter 5: Only God Is Entitled

1. Tozer, A.W. *This World: Playground or Battleground?* Christian Publications.com: Christian Publications, Inc., 1988. (Italics mine).

2. Beecher, Henry Ward. *Henry Ward Beecher: An American Portrait.* The Readers Club, 1942.

Chapter 6: Time Can Be on Your Side

1. Kahn, Alice. *Multiple Sarcasm.* Berkeley: 10 Speed Press, 1984.

2. Penn, William. *Some Fruits of Solitude.* Friends United Press, 1978.

3. Bercot, David W. *The Kingdom That Turned The World Upside Down* (Page 36). Tyler, TX: Scroll Publishing, 2003.

4. Aurelius, Marcus. *The Meditations of Marcus Aurelius.* New York: Collier & Son Company, 1909.

Chapter 7: Jesus is Perfect and I Don't Love Him Enough

1. Inspired by a sermon delivered by Stan Addis entitled, *Why Jesus.* Indianapolis, March 20, 1998.

Chapter 8: Only the King Can Give Us the Crown of Contentment

1. Lewis, C.S. *Mere Christianity.* New York: Harper Collins publishers, 2001.

Chapter 11: We Can Wake up from the American Dream

1. Plato. *Plato's Complete Works.* Littlefield, Adams and Company, 1959.

2. Lewis, C.S. *Mere Christianity.* New York: Harper Collins publishers, 2001.

3. *Ante-Nicene Fathers.* Edited by Alexander Roberts, D.D. & James Donaldson, LL.D. Peabody, MA: Hendrickson Publishers, Inc., 1994.

4. Bercot, David W. *The Kingdom That Turned The World Upside Down* (Page 35, 36). Tyler, TX: Scroll Publishing Company, 2003.

Chapter 14: Talk to Someone Who Cares

1. Tozer, A.W. *This World: Playground or Battleground?* Christianpublications.com: Christian Publications, Inc., 1988.

Chapter 15: Trust in God's Uncommon Sense

1. Swindoll, Charles. *Intimacy With The Almighty.* Thomas Nelson Jack Countryman, 2000

2. Bach, Richard David. *Jonathan Livingston Seagull.* Scribner Book Company, 1970.

Chapter 16: Politically Content

1. Buckley, William F. *Up From Liberalism.* Arlington House Books, 1968.

2. Shtern, Liudmila. *Joseph Brodsky: A Personal Memoir.* Baskerville Publishers, 2004.

3. Bercot, David W. *A Dictionary of Early Christian Beliefs* (Tertullian, page 545). Peabody, MA: Hendrickson Publishers, Inc., 1998.

4. Bercot, David W. *A Dictionary of Early Christian Beliefs* (Tertullian, page 545). Peabody, MA: Hendrickson Publishers, Inc., 1998. (Italics mine).

Chapter 17: Jesus Doesn't Need to Be Converted

1. Tozer, A.W. *This World: Playground or Battleground?* Christianpublications.com: Christian Publications, 1988.

2. *From The Pastor of Hermas, Ante-Nicene Fathers,* Volume 2:49.

3. From Clement of Alexandria's *Maximus Sermon,* quoted in the *Ante-Nicene Fathers,* Volume 2:58.

4. From Cyprian, *on the Glory of Martyrdom, Ante-Nicene Fathers,* Volume 5:586.

5. From *The Treatises of Cyprian, Ante-Nicene Fathers,* Volume 5:431.

6. From the *Stromata, Ante-Nicene Fathers,* Volume 2:379.

7. From *The Writings of Tertullian, Ante-Nicene Fathers,* Volume 6:77.

Chapter 18: The Truth Doesn't Have to Hurt

1. Churchill, Winston. *Churchill Speaks: Winston S. Churchill in Peace and War: Collected Speeches, 1897–1963.* Atheneum, 1981.

2. Churchill, Winston. *Churchill Speaks: Winston S. Churchill in Peace and War: Collected Speeches, 1897–1963.* Atheneum, 1981.

Chapter 19: What Do I Know?

1. Socrates, *The Dialogues of Plato.* New York: Liveright Publishing, 1927.

2. Van Gogh, Vincent. *Dear Theo.* New York: Penguin Group, 1995.

3. Washington, James Melvin. *A Testament of Hope: The Essential Writings & Speeches of Martin Luther king Jr.* New York: Harper Collins Publishers, 1991.

4. Plutarch. *Plutarch Moralia.* Cambridge, MA: Harvard University Press, 1959.

5. Kempis, Thomas A. *of the Imitation of Christ.* New Kensington, PA: Whitaker House, 1981.

6. Bercot, David W. *The Kingdom That Turned The World Upside Down* (Pages 145–148). Tyler, TX: Scroll Publishing Company, 2003.

Chapter 20: Everything Gets Old Except God

1. Donne, John. *John Donne—The Major Works: Including Songs and Sonnets and Sermons.* New York: Oxford University Press, Inc., 1990.

2. Huxley, Thomas H. *T.H. Huxley's Diary of the Voyage of H M S Rattlesnake.* New York: Doubleday, Doran and Company, Inc., 1935.

3. Berlioz, Hector. *The Memoirs of Hector Berlioz.* Everyman's Library, 2002.

4. Bach, Richard David. *Jonathan Livingston Seagull.* Scribner Book Company, 1970.

Chapter 21: The Passionless

1. From the *Address of Tatian to the Greeks, Ante-Nicene Fathers,* Volume 2:69.

2. From *The Treatises of Cyprian, Ante-Nicene Fathers,* Volume 5:473.

3. Kempis, Thomas A. *of the Imitation of Christ.* New Kensington, PA: Whitaker House, 1981.

4. Kempis, Thomas A. *of the Imitation of Christ.* New Kensington, PA: Whitaker House, 1981.

5. Kempis, Thomas A. *of the Imitation of Christ.* New Kensington, PA: Whitaker House, 1981.

Chapter 22: Simplicity Is Flexible

1. Kempis, Thomas A. *of the Imitation of Christ.* New Kensington, PA: Whitaker House, 1981.

Chapter 23: You've Got the Wants

1. Socrates, *The Dialogues of Plato.* New York: Liveright Publishing, 1927.

Chapter 24: American Idols

1. Tozer, A.W. *This World: Playground or Battleground?* Christianpublications.com: Christian Publications, Inc., 1988.

2. From *The Writings of Tertullian, Ante-Nicene Fathers,* Volume 3:69.

Epilogue:

1. Thoreau, Henry David. *Walden.* New York: Houghton Mifflin Company, 1949

This and other quality books are available from

OverLookedBooks

Visit us online at:
www.overlookedbooks.com

Printed in the United States
58706LVS00003B/534

9 781595 940698